Microsoft®

Deploying Microsoft® Forefront® Threat Management Gateway 2010

W0007989

Yuri Diogenes
Dr. Thomas W. Shinder

PUBLISHED BY
Microsoft Press
A Division of Microsoft Corporation
One Microsoft Way
Redmond, Washington 98052-6399

Library of Congress Control Number: 2010938148

Printed and bound in the United States of America.

Microsoft Press books are available through booksellers and distributors worldwide. For further information about international editions, contact your local Microsoft Corporation office or contact Microsoft Press International directly at fax (425) 936-7329. Visit our Web site at www.microsoft.com/mspress. Send comments to mspinput@ microsoft.com.

Microsoft and the trademarks listed at http://www.microsoft.com/about/legal/en/us/IntellectualProperty /Trademarks/EN-US.aspx are trademarks of the Microsoft group of companies. All other marks are property of their respective owners.

The example companies, organizations, products, domain names, e-mail addresses, logos, people, places, and events depicted herein are fictitious. No association with any real company, organization, product, domain name, e-mail address, logo, person, place, or event is intended or should be inferred.

Acqulsitions Editor: Devon Musgrave
Developmental Editor: Karen Szall
Project Editor: Karen Szall
Editorial Production: nSight, Inc.
Technical Reviewer: Mitch Tulloch; Technical Review services provided by Content Master, a member of CM Group, Ltd.
Cover: Tom Draper Design

Body Part No. X17-15053

Contents

What do you think of this book? We want to hear from you!

Microsoft is interested in hearing your feedback so we can continually improve our books and learning
resources for you. To participate in a brief online survey, please visit:

www.microsoft.com/learning/booksurvey/

What do you think of this book? We want to hear from you!

Microsoft is interested in hearing your feedback so we can continually improve our books and learning resources for you. To participate in a brief online survey, please visit:

www.microsoft.com/learning/booksurvey/

Acknowledgments

This Forefront project took almost a year to write and resulted in three separate books about deploying Forefront products. Although the authors get lots of credit, there can be little doubt that we could not have even begun, much less completed, this book without the cooperation (not to mention the permission) of an incredibly large number of people.

It's here that we'd like to take a few moments of your time to express our gratitude to the folks who made it all possible.

With thanks...

To the folks at Microsoft Press who made the process as smooth as they possibly could: Karen Szall, Devon Musgrave, and their crew.

To the TMG Product Team folks, especially to Ori Yosefi and David Strausberg, for helping us by reviewing the Service Pack 1 chapter. To all our friends from CSS Security, especially to Bala Natarajan for reviewing content.

From Yuri

First and foremost to God, for blessing my life, leading my way, and giving me the strength to take on the challenges as just another step in life. To my eternal supporter in all moments of my life: my wife Alexsandra. To my daughters who, although very young, understand when I close the office door and say, "I'm really busy." Thanks for understanding. I love you, Yanne and Ysis.

To my friend Thomas Shinder, whom I was fortunate enough to meet three years ago. Thanks for shaping my writing skills and also contributing to my personal grown with your thoughts, advice, and guidance. Without a doubt, these long months working on this project were worth it because of our amazing partnership. I can't forget to thank the two other friends who wrote the *Microsoft Forefront Threat Management Gateway Administrator's Companion* with me: Jim Harrison and Mohit Saxena. They were, without a doubt, the pillars for this writing career in which I'm now fully engaged. Thanks, guys. To, as Jim says, "da Boyz": Tim "Thor" Mullen, Steve Moffat, and Greg Mulholland. You guys are amazing. Thanks for sharing all the tales.

To my friend Thomas Detzner and all ISA/TMG EMEA engineers (including the great folks from PFE), thanks for sharing your knowledge and all the partnerships that we have had over these years. I would also like to say thanks to all my friends from Microsoft CSS Security (in Texas, North Carolina, and Washington) for sharing experiences every day, with a special thanks to all the great engineers from CSS India—you guys are the pillars of this team. Thanks for pushing me with tough questions and concerns. To all the readers of my articles and blogs, thanks for all the feedback that you guys share with me. If I keep writing in my spare time, it is because I know you are reading it. To all the Forefront MVPs, keep up the amazing job that you guys do. Last, but not least, to my buddies Mohit Kumar, Alexandre Hollanda, Daniel Mauser, and Alejandro Leal, for your consistent support throughout the years.

From Tom

As Yuri does, I acknowledge the blessings from God, who took "a fool like me" and guided me on a path that I never would have chosen on my own. The second most important acknowledgement I must make is to my beautiful wife, Deb Shinder, whom I consider my hand of God. Without her, I don't know where I would be today, except that I know that the place wouldn't be anywhere near as good as the place I am now.

I also want to acknowledge my good friend Yuri Diogenes, my co-writer on this project. Yuri really held this project together. I had just started working for Microsoft and was learning about the ins and outs of the Microsoft system, and I was also taking on a lot of detailed and complex projects alongside the writing of this book. Yuri helped keep me focused, spent a lot of time pointing me in the right direction, and essentially is responsible for enabling me to get done what I needed to get done. I have no doubt that, without Yuri guiding this effort, it probably never would have been completed.

Props go out to Jim Harrison, "the King of TMG," as well as to Greg Mulholland, Steve Moffat, and Tim Mullen. You guys were the moral authority that drove us to completion. I also want to give a special "shout out" to Mohit Saxena. His TMG chops and sense of humor also helped us over the finish line.

Finally, I want to thank the operators of ISAserver.org and all the members of the ISAserver.org community. You guys were the spark that started a flaming hot career for me with ISA Server and then TMG. You guys are a never-ending inspiration and a demonstration of the power of community and ways communities can work together to solve hard problems and share solutions.

Introduction

When we began this project, our intent was to create a real world scenario that would guide IT professionals in using Microsoft best practices to deploy Microsoft Forefront Threat Management Gateway (TMG) 2010. We hope you find that we have achieved that goal. We've also included the main deployment scenarios for Forefront TMG, and we take a deep dive into the installation process from the RTM version to the Service Pack 1 version.

This book provides administrative procedures, tested design examples, quick answers, and tips. In addition, it covers some of the most common deployment scenarios and describes ways to take full advantage of the product's capabilities. This book covers pre-deployment tasks, use of Forefront TMG in a Secure Web Gateway Scenario, software and hardware requirements, and installation and configuration, using best practice recommendations.

Who Is This Book For?

Deploying Microsoft Forefront Threat Management Gateway 2010 covers the planning and deployment phases for this product. This book is designed for:

- Administrators who are deploying Forefront TMG
- Administrators who are experienced with Windows Server 2008 in general and with Windows networking in particular
- Current ISA Server administrators
- Administrators who are new to Forefront TMG
- Technology specialists, such as security administrators and network administrators

Because this book is limited in size and we want to provide you the maximum value, we assume a basic knowledge of Windows Server 2008 and Windows networking. These technologies are not discussed in detail, but this book contains material on both of these topics that relates to Forefront TMG administrative tasks.

How Is This Book Organized?

Deploying Microsoft Forefront Threat Management Gateway 2010 is written to be a deployment guide and also to be a source of architectural information related to the product. The book is organized in such a way that you can follow the steps to plan and deploy the product. The steps are based on a deployment scenario for the company Contoso. As you go through the steps, you will also notice tips for best practices implementation. At the end of each chapter, you will see an "Administrator's Punch List," in which you will find a summary of the main administrative tasks that were covered throughout the chapter. This is a quick checklist to help you review the main deployment tasks.

The book is organized into three chapters: Chapter 1, "Understanding Forefront Threat Management Gateway 2010," introduces you to the core concepts of firewalls, perimeter protection, and proxies and guides you through the use of Forefront TMG as a secure web gateway. Chapter 2, "Installing and Configuring Forefront Threat Management Gateway 2010," guides you through the product's installation and configuration. Chapter 3, "Deploying Forefront 2010 Service Pack 1," covers the new features of Service Pack 1 and describes how to install and configure those features.

We really hope you find *Deploying Microsoft Threat Management Gateway 2010* useful and accurate. We have an open door policy for email at *mspress.tmgbook@tacteam.net*, and you can contact us through our personal blogs and Twitter accounts:

- *http://blogs.technet.com/yuridiogenes* and *http://blogs.technet.com /tomshinder*

- *http://twitter.com/yuridiogenes* and *http://twitter.com/tshinder*

Support for This Book

Every effort has been made to ensure the accuracy of this book. As corrections or changes are collected, they will be added to the O'Reilly Media website. To find Microsoft Press book and media corrections:

1. Go to *http://microsoftpress.oreilly.com*.

2. In the Search box, type the ISBN for the book and click Search.

3. Select the book from the search results, which will take you to the book's catalog page.

4. On the book's catalog page, under the picture of the book cover, click View/Submit Errata.

If you have questions regarding the book or the companion content that are not answered by visiting the book's catalog page, please send them to Microsoft Press by sending an email message to *mspinput@microsoft.com*.

We Want to Hear from You

We welcome your feedback about this book. Please share your comments and ideas through the following short survey:

http://www.microsoft.com/learning/booksurvey

Your participation helps Microsoft Press create books that better meet your needs and your standards.

> **NOTE** We hope that you will give us detailed feedback in our survey. If you have questions about our publishing program, upcoming titles, or Microsoft Press in general, we encourage you to interact with us using Twitter at *http://twitter.com/MicrosoftPress*. For support issues, use only the email address shown earlier.

CHAPTER 1

Understanding Forefront Threat Management Gateway 2010

F orefront Threat Management Gateway (TMG) 2010 plays a key role in overall network protection, helping to secure Web access and Web publishing. Forefront TMG has a comprehensive set of features that goes beyond the traditional firewall role, focusing more on the application layer and enhancing network-level protection.

A History of Perimeter Protection

Forefront Threat Management Gateway (Forefront TMG) 2010 is the latest version of Microsoft's network firewall, Web proxy and VPN server. Previous versions of the product included Microsoft Proxy Server 1.0, Proxy Server 2.0, Microsoft Internet Security and Acceleration (ISA) Server 2000, ISA Server 2004 and ISA Server 2006. The first two versions of the product, Proxy Server 1.0 and Proxy Server 2.0, were primarily focused on providing forward proxy capabilities and required that other network firewalls be in place to protect the Proxy Server-based Web proxy solution.

A major change took place with the introduction of ISA Server 2000. This was the first version of the product that could be considered an enterprise-ready, network layer firewall. ISA Server 2000 was the first version of the product to provide both stateful packet inspection and application layer inspection. However, ISA Server 2000 was built on a network security model that was popular in the 1990s, namely, the concept of having a "trusted" internal (corporate) network and an "untrusted" external (public) network.

The problem with ISA Server 2000 was that, as we entered the twenty-first century, the concept of trusted internal and untrusted external networks was no longer valid.

Studies and reports showed that attacks emanating from internal networks were as dangerous and destructive as those coming from the outside. To respond to such threats, ISA Server 2004 was released, which used a new networking model in which *no* networks were considered trusted. Out of the box, no network traffic could traverse the ISA 2004 firewall. Only after the ISA firewall administrator explicitly configured firewall rules could traffic move through the firewall. In addition, the concept of all networks being untrusted was extended to VPN client connections, as well as site-to-site VPN gateway links.

Even more significant in the introduction of the ISA 2004 firewall was its ability to perform stateful packet inspection and application layer inspection over *all* connections to and through the firewall. This meant that stateful packet inspection and application layer inspection was performed on outgoing connections, incoming connections, remote access VPN connections, and site-to-site VPN connections. This powerful packet and application layer inspection on all connections was the natural extension of the idea that "no networks can be trusted."

The next version of the ISA firewall, ISA Server 2006, was an upgrade focused on Web publishing, or what is often referred to as "reverse Web proxy." New features, such as Kerberos-constrained delegation and advanced two-factor authentication methods, were included in the 2006 version of the ISA firewall. However, little was done to advance the product's outbound access control and security feature set.

This state of affairs turns around significantly with the introduction of the latest version of the Microsoft's enterprise-grade firewall, Forefront Threat Management Gateway 2010. In contrast to ISA 2006, major investments have been made to make Forefront TMG the premiere outbound access control and Web security solution. These investments are seen in the new features included with the Forefront TMG firewall, some of which include:

- The Network Inspection System (NIS)
- Outbound SSL Inspection (outbound SSL-to-SSL bridging)
- Web anti-malware inspection (antivirus/anti-malware)
- URL filtering
- An Advanced Web Access Control policies wizard

These and other new features make Forefront TMG the ideal outbound access solution. However, in contrast to ISA 2006, in which major investments (in terms of new reverse proxy features) were made for inbound access control, very little has been done in Forefront TMG in terms of improvements for inbound access control. The major exception to this is support for the Secure Socket Tunneling Protocol (SSTP) for remote access VPN client connections and the addition of NAP Integration. You will not see any other major changes in the Web or Server Publishing features when moving from ISA 2006 to Forefront TMG.

The reason for Forefront TMG's focus on outbound access control is that the majority of inbound access (remote access) effort is going into the Microsoft Forefront Unified Access Gateway (UAG) 2010. At this point in time, it is expected that Forefront TMG will be used primarily for outbound access control and network firewall, and UAG will be used for inbound access (remote access) control.

Forefront TMG as a Perimeter Network Device

The Forefront TMG firewall was built from the ground up to be an edge network firewall. With powerful stateful packet and application layer inspection features and capabilities, the ISA firewall, and now the Forefront TMG firewall, have both proven themselves time and again to be highly resilient to attack. Together they have one of the best track records for security in the entire firewall industry. This track record is demonstrated by the very small number of reported security issues found in the ISA or Forefront TMG firewall code when compared to similar products.

However, Forefront TMG is not only an edge firewall. In fact, it might be more accurate to think of the Forefront TMG firewall as a "perimeter security device." As a perimeter security device, the Forefront TMG firewall fits in nicely in a number of perimeter security scenarios:

- At the edge of the corporate network
- As a back-end firewall behind another Forefront TMG firewall or third-party firewall
- As a parallel firewall on the edge, next to another Forefront TMG or third-party firewall
- As a network service segment firewall, providing a secure perimeter between client systems and network services
- As a multi-homed firewall that acts as the hub between multiple internal and perimeter networks

You can place Forefront TMG as a network perimeter firewall in any collection of systems that represents different security zones to protect, record, and report on the traffic moving between those systems.

As a network perimeter security device, the Forefront TMG firewall can actually act in one or more of several roles. Both ISA Server and Forefront TMG are often referred to as the "Swiss Army Knife of network firewalls." The reason for this is that Forefront TMG can act as and provide the following services:

- A network firewall
- A forward and reverse Web proxy server and a Winsock proxy server
- A Web caching server
- A remote access VPN server
- A Site-to-Site VPN Gateway
- A secure email gateway

Network Firewall

As a network firewall, Forefront TMG provides protection for itself and for any network behind the firewall. Forefront TMG uses advanced stateful packet and application layer inspection capabilities to help secure the traffic that moves to and through the firewall. This helps ensure that both traditional network layer attacks that were popular in the past and the crop of application layer attacks that are popular now are blocked by the firewall before they reach their intended destinations.

As a network firewall, Forefront TMG can be placed on the edge of the network, with a connection directly on the Internet, or it can be placed behind other firewalls so that it becomes the perimeter firewall for the network segments that lie behind it. This allows your Forefront TMG firewall to be the central "choke point" and observe all traffic moving between secured segments, a duty common to all network firewalls.

Forward and Reverse Proxy, Web Proxy, and Winsock Proxy Server

Web proxy servers are used to control HTTP and HTTPS connections between two network hosts. The Forefront TMG firewall can act as both a forward and a reverse proxy server. In its role as a Web proxy server, the Web proxy client actually sends the request to the Web proxy server. The Web proxy evaluates the request and, if the request is allowed, recreates the request on behalf of the requesting client and forwards it to the destination server. The destination server then replies, and the reply is forwarded to the requesting client. This is typically referred to as "forward proxy."

In addition to forward Web proxy services, the Forefront TMG firewall can also provide reverse proxy services. In this scenario, Forefront TMG accepts HTTP or HTTPS requests from external hosts. The connection is terminated on the external interface of the Forefront TMG firewall and inspected. If the connection is allowed, it is recreated on behalf of the external requesting client and forwarded to the "published" Web server. The published Web server responds to the request, Forefront TMG intercepts the response, and, if the response is considered valid, the request is forwarded to the requesting client.

 SECURITY ALERT Many types of malware take advantage of SSL to hide themselves from network security device detection. Attackers are able to take advantage of SSL to move malware into your network and private corporate data out of your network, because most perimeter security devices are unable to evaluate the contents of an SSL-encrypted session.

In both forward and reverse proxy scenarios the Forefront TMG firewall is able to perform application layer inspection to help ensure that there are no dangerous commands or payloads in the communication. For forward proxy connections, Forefront TMG is able to take advantage of its new Web anti-malware capabilities, as well as its URL filtering. Both forward and reverse proxy scenarios benefit from SSL bridging, which helps prevent exploits from being hidden from within an SSL tunnel. Also, both forward and reverse proxy scenarios support HTTP protocol inspection, which helps you control the HTTP commands and headers that are allowed through the TMG Web application firewall.

Web Caching Server

As an extension of its Web proxy feature set, Forefront TMG can perform both forward and reverse Web caching. In a forward caching scenario, a Web proxy client on a Forefront TMG-protected network makes a request for content from a Web server by going through the Forefront TMG firewall. Forefront TMG proxies the request to the destination Web server and receives the response. Before forwarding the response to the requesting client, Forefront TMG places the content in its in-memory cache and then moves it to its on-disk cache. After placing the content in the cache, the content is returned to the requesting client.

Forward caching has the end result of reducing the overall bandwidth used on the Internet link by providing content from cache instead of from the destination Web server. In addition, the end-user experience is significantly improved because content is returned at LAN speed instead of at relatively slow WAN speed.

Reverse caching enables Forefront TMG to cache content requested by external clients that is returned by published Web servers. In this scenario, the external client makes a request for content on a Web server on a network protected by Forefront TMG. Forefront TMG intercepts the request, evaluates it, and then, if it is acceptable, forwards it to the published Web server. The Web server returns the response, Forefront TMG intercepts it, evaluates it, and then, for content that is marked as cacheable, Forefront TMG will cache the content in memory, and subsequently on disk, and forward the response to the external requesting client.

Administrators Insight

The end result of reverse caching is a bit different from that of forward caching and adds different value. While forward caching reduces overall Internet bandwidth usage and improves the overall end-user experience, reverse caching has little effect on Internet bandwidth and no effect on the end-user experience. Instead, reverse caching enables you to reduce the load on the published Web server, and, in some scenarios, enables you to allow external users access to content on the published Web server, even when the Web server is disabled or down for maintenance. In addition, it can reduce the amount of bandwidth usage on networks between the TMG firewall and the published Web servers.

Remote Access VPN Server

Forefront TMG has advanced VPN server capabilities that provide you with granular control over what remote access VPN clients can do when they are connected to your network. Forefront TMG can act as a VPN termination point for two types of VPN connections: remote access VPN clients and site-to-site VPN gateway connections.

A remote access VPN client is a client system that uses a network layer VPN protocol to connect to the VPN server. When the remote access client connects to the remote access VPN server, that client has access to resources behind the VPN server. For remote access VPN clients and servers, there is a one-to-one relationship between the client and the server. This is in contrast to the role of the VPN gateway, which is covered in the next section of this chapter.

The remote access VPN client has a virtual link layer connection to the corporate network. This provides an experience similar to that seen by hosts that are either physically or wirelessly connected at the corporate network. VPN clients use the Internet as their transport to the corporate network. Once they are connected, VPN client systems can access resources on the corporate network in a way that is similar to the way an on-network host works.

However, VPN clients pose a challenge that you typically do not see for on-network hosts: Most VPN clients are unmanaged clients with unknown security status. Because you don't know how secure or unsecure remote access clients might be, you need to take extra precautions before confidently allowing any host to be a remote access VPN client.

Forefront TMG solves some of the issues related to the questionable security status of a VPN client by enabling the following features:

- **Granular access controls to control the server and protocols VPN clients can reach** VPN clients can only reach the servers you want them to reach, and can only use the protocols you want them to use when connecting to those servers.

- **Stateful packet and application layer inspection on all traffic moving through the remote access VPN link** This helps prevent exploits from being transferred from a compromised VPN client into the corporate network.

- **User-based access controls on VPN client connections** Because the Forefront TMG firewall is aware of the user context of the connection (based on the user who established the VPN connection), the firewall is able to enable access to servers and protocols and applications based on user name or user group membership.

- **Support for Remote Access Quarantine Control and Network Access Protection (NAP)** Remote Access Quarantine Control and NAP enable you to test the security configuration of a remote access VPN client before giving it access to resources on the corporate network. If the remote access VPN client fails to pass security checks, then it may be offered a method of remediation. Only after the remote access VPN client passes your security checks will it be allowed access to resources you've designated on the corporate network.

Forefront TMG supports several network-layer VPN protocols:

- SSTP
- PPTP
- L2TP/IPsec

SSTP support is new in Forefront TMG. With SSTP, users can establish remote access VPN client connections from virtually anywhere. This is made possible by encapsulating the VPN communications in an HTTP header that is secured by SSL. Since almost all firewalls and Web proxies allow outbound access to HTTPS, SSTP clients can establish connections from locations that have port limiting firewalls or Web proxies only. This enables SSTP client connectivity from locations where PPTP and L2TP/IPsec are likely to fail.

Site-to-Site VPN Gateway

Remote access VPN clients have a one-to-one relationship with the remote access VPN server. This means that the remote access VPN client has a single connection to the VPN server; that connection is between the client and the remote access VPN server.

In contrast, the site-to-site VPN gateway has a one-to-many relationship with clients. A single remote access gateway link can have many clients behind it. In effect, the remote access gateway is a VPN router that connects to other VPN routers over the Internet. Remote access VPN gateways allow you to create virtual network segments over the Internet. However, unlike internal network segments that are connected by LAN routers and switches, clients on remote networks are connected to the corporate network over the VPN gateway.

For example, suppose you have a network in Dallas and another in Seattle. You want machines on each of the networks to have access to resources on the other network. There are a number of ways you can do this, such as using a dedicated WAN link to connect the offices. The problem with dedicated WAN links is that they're typically slow, expensive, or both. Site-to-site VPN gateways can solve both these problems by using the Internet as a transport and creating a virtual link layer connection between the two networks.

Forefront TMG can be used as a VPN gateway to connect to other Forefront TMG VPN gateways, it can connect to ISA Server VPN gateways, and it can even connect to third-party VPN gateways. Like all other connectivity methods available with Forefront TMG, all connections made through the site-to-site VPN link are exposed to Forefront TMG 's stateful packet and application layer inspection mechanisms, which help ensure that connections made over the link are secure and reduces the probability that one office will share exploits with another office.

The same granular access controls that are available for remote access VPN clients are also available when using Forefront TMG as a site-to-site VPN gateway. However, for site-to-site VPN gateway deployments, only the following VPN protocols are available:

- L2TP/IPsec
- PPTP
- IPSec tunnel mode

L2TP/IPsec is usually the preferred method because it provides the best performance and manageability features. PPTP is preferred at times, because it requires a low overhead to get a solution working, while IPsec tunnel mode should be reserved for situations in which you want to connect the Forefront TMG VPN gateway to a third-party VPN gateway.

Secure Email Gateway

Forefront TMG introduces an entirely new feature set that is part of its email gateway solution. If you are an experienced ISA Server administrator, you might remember that previous versions of the ISA firewall had what was called the "SMTP Message Screener." The SMTP Message Screener provided some rudimentary email support by allowing you to control which email messages were allowed through the ISA firewall to a published SMTP server. Areas of control revolved around keywords, attachment names and extensions, and source and destination user names or domains.

The SMTP Message Screener was included with ISA Server 2000, but was dropped in subsequent versions of the product. SMTP email hygiene support returns with Forefront TMG. However, instead of a basic solution like that provided by the SMTP Message Screener, Forefront TMG offers a powerful, enterprise-ready email security solution in its role as an SMTP email gateway. The Forefront TMG email gateway feature is powered by the Edge Transport Server role of Exchange Server 2010 together with Microsoft Forefront Protection 2010 for Exchange Server. The Edge Transport Server role provides key features, such as connection filtering and spam detection, while the Forefront Protection for Exchange (FPE) components protect against malware or other dangerous code entering or leaving your network.

In addition to providing an on-premises solution for email hygiene, the Forefront TMG Secure Email Gateway role can inspect email moving both inbound to your corporate email servers and outbound to other mail servers. Thus, the solution protects you from exploits carried out by others and protects others from exploits that might originate within your organization.

Administrator Insight

Many administrators have been told that the Exchange Edge Server role is not supported on domain member machines. While this is a strong recommendation of the Exchange Server team, because the Exchange Edge Server doesn't have an advanced firewall installed on it, the scenario changes when the Exchange Edge Server role is installed on the TMG firewall. In this case, it is safe to make the TMG firewall that hosts the Exchange Edge Server role a domain member.

The following sections provide more detail about some of the features included in Forefront TMG that weren't available in ISA Server.

Forefront TMG as a Secure Web Gateway

Forefront TMG has capabilities that can be used in many edge scenarios, as explained earlier in this chapter. One of the strongest and most commonly used scenarios for Forefront TMG is the secure Web gateway. There are many challenges in the secure Web access area and

Forefront TMG has many features that can overcome those challenges. However, before going into more detail about those features, we will analyze the core secure Web access needs from both the user's and the enterprise's perspectives. To better understand this idea, review the points in the scenario displayed in Figure 1-1.

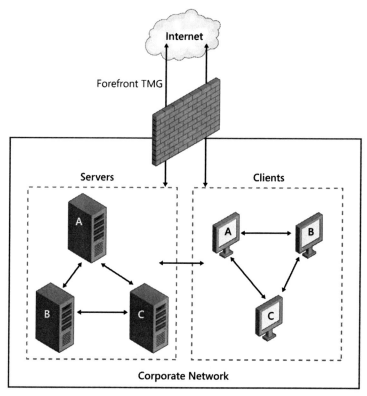

FIGURE 1-1

In the scenario depicted in Figure 1-1, you have:

- **Outbound access from servers** Servers usually have special needs for Internet access. Sometimes the company security policy only allows access from the server to some specific Web sites, such as Windows Update. Forefront TMG can address this need by controlling access to a specific group of servers.

- **Communication between servers and clients** Most of the available secure Web access gateways are aligned to address only outbound access controls. Forefront TMG can go beyond that and also identify malicious access attempts between computers (servers to servers, servers to client, or client to client). This capability is part of a feature called the Network Inspection System (NIS).

- **Outbound access from clients** Client workstations also have special needs for Internet access. Forefront TMG can protect Internet access for workstations by using many of the secure Web gateway features, such as malware inspection, URL filtering, and HTTPS inspection.

Now that you understand the core Web access protection scenarios, we will look at the features mentioned in each scenario in more detail.

Network Inspection System

Network Inspection System (NIS) is one of the features of the Intrusion Prevention System (IPS) in Forefront TMG. NIS uses signatures of known vulnerabilities from the Microsoft Malware Protection Center (MMPC) to help detect malicious traffic and then to take action (which might be to block the traffic) when an exploit is detected. Figure 1-2 shows the NIS interface on Forefront TMG.

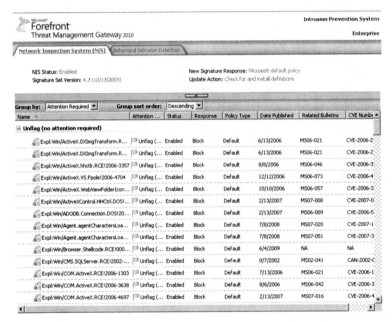

FIGURE 1-2

NIS uses the Generic Application Protocol Analyzer (GAPA) engine. The goal of GAPA is to build an IPS that is aware of the application protocol that it is inspecting and able to apply complex conditions or rules to the intercepted network traffic. These conditions rely on the logical structure of the protocol under inspection. The NIS engine is integrated into the firewall binaries, although it also has dynamic engine loading capabilities. The engine loads a snapshot file on each reload configuration, which contains the engine signatures and protocol definitions. Signatures are downloaded from Microsoft Update Center both on a regular basis and during emergencies, so that NIS can respond to zero-day attacks. Figure 1-3 illustrates how snapshots and engine updates are managed.

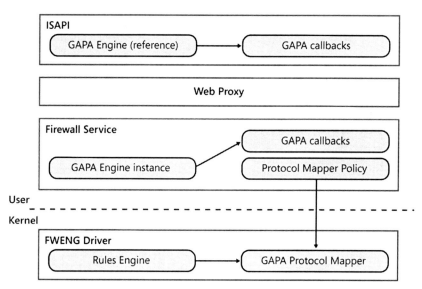

FIGURE 1-3

NIS allows Forefront TMG to act as an intrusion prevention system, which goes beyond the traditional secure Web access gateway and adds another layer of protection to the edge.

> **NOTE** For more information on how to configure NIS on Forefront TMG, read Chapter 13 of the *Microsoft Forefront Threat Management Gateway (TMG) Administrator's Companion* book from Microsoft Press.

Malware Inspection

As new threats are getting smarter and are leaving the network layer and moving to the application layer, the challenge of keeping all workstations behind the edge device updated with the latest antivirus signature is getting even more difficult. Beyond that, there are always scenarios in which unmanaged workstations need to cross the enterprise's network boundaries for Internet access. The core advantages of inspecting traffic against malware at the edge are:

- It is easier to keep the edge updated with malware signatures.
- Unmanaged machines that might not have host antivirus applications installed are also protected.
- Malware activity detected on the edge can be easily monitored using built-in logging and reporting options.

The main purpose of the edge malware inspection feature in Forefront TMG is to inspect Web traffic on the edge to prevent any malware (viruses or spyware) from infecting the computers located inside the organization.

The Malware Inspection filter (also known as the EMP filter, which stands for Edge Malware Protection) is a built-in Web filter that intercepts outbound HTTP traffic and submits it for scanning to the Microsoft malware protection engine (MPEngine.dll). Malware inspection can be enabled globally in the Web access policy, as shown in Figure 1-4.

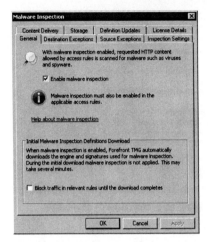

FIGURE 1-4

The malware protection engine needs the full file to scan its content for malware; therefore the filter will accumulate the file content in order to be able to perform the scan. This can introduce some problems (such as degraded user experience) related to the delay caused by the accumulation. Forefront TMG 2010 uses different delivery methods to protect the user experience when downloading files from the Internet:

- **Delayed download** If the delay caused by data accumulation and inspection is longer than an established threshold, the trickling or HTML progress page methods will be used by the malware inspection filter to deliver the content to the client.

- **HTML progress page** This method uses an HTML page, returned by Forefront TMG to the client browser, which informs the user that the requested content is being inspected; the page displays an indicator of the download and inspection progress.

- **Trickling** This method is intended to be used in cases where the "delayed download" method has reached the time threshold and the HTML progress page doesn't apply.

- **Fast trickling** Forefront TMG sends the data as fast as possible to the user, but holds back the last part in order to complete the scan before completing the transfer.

Malware inspection is a key secure Web gateway feature that Forefront TMG uses to protect internal workstations.

HTTPS Inspection

Throughout the years, end users were told that to securely transfer confidential data on the Internet, they needed to only trust sites that used HTTPS. Users got more conscious about e-commerce and carefully looked at the lock in the Web browser to see if that traffic was encrypted. This is indeed a great habit that took years to build; however, there are challenges in this area because encrypted traffic that crosses the firewall is not inspected. The dangerous part of this is that it relies on the legitimacy of the Web site that the user is trying to access. If the destination Web site is using this encrypted channel to transfer malware, the traditional edge device will not be able to inspect the traffic and identify it. Figure 1-5 shows the traditional HTTPS access from client to destination Web server, crossing an edge device.

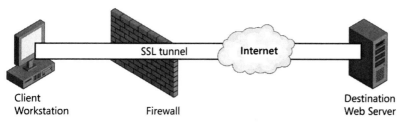

FIGURE 1-5

Forefront TMG introduces a new feature called HTTPS inspection, which allows Forefront TMG to inspect the HTTPS traffic and identify malware. HTTPS inspection on Forefront TMG is based on a trusted man-in-the-middle mechanism, in which Forefront TMG works as a trusted man in the middle to be the SSL site for the client. Figure 1-6 shows how Forefront TMG performs HTTPS inspection.

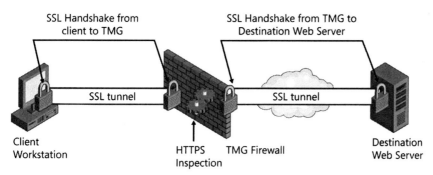

FIGURE 1-6

The HTTPS inspection feature can be enabled using the Web Access Policy Wizard, from the Web Access Settings area or from the Web Protection Tasks. When enabled, this feature will show the Enable HTTPS Inspection option for globally enabling HTTPS inspection, as shown in Figure 1-7.

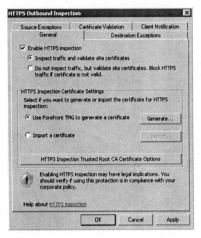

FIGURE 1-7

NOTE For more information on how to configure HTTPS inspection on Forefront TMG, read Chapter 20, "HTTP and HTTPS Inspection," in *Microsoft Forefront Threat Management Gateway (TMG) Administrator's Companion*, from Microsoft Press.

HTTPS inspection is not restricted to determining whether the content within the packet includes malware or not; it also enables:

- Certificate validation (confirms that the destination server certificate is valid)
- Certificate generation and deployment
- Source and destinations exception lists (allows the administrator to create exceptions for SSL inspection)
- Client notifications

NOTE There are some caveats when enabling HTTPS Inspection on Forefront TMG. For more information about the most common problems, read "Common Problems while Implementing HTTPS Inspection on Forefront TMG 2010 RC," at *http://blogs.technet.com /isablog/archive/2009/10/19/common-problems-while-implementing-https-inspection-on -forefront-tmg-2010-rc.aspx.*

URL Filtering

URL Filtering allows you to control users' access to Web sites and protects the organization by denying access to known malicious sites and to sites displaying inappropriate or pornographic materials, based on predefined URL categories. Forefront TMG uses information obtained from Microsoft Reputation Service (MRS), which is a cloud-based service hosted by Microsoft to categorize URLs.

The MRS team wanted to confront an inherent problem with traditional URL Filtering solutions: The problem domain is simply too large for any single vendor to provide a complete solution. As a result, there are multiple vendors who each specialize in a specific area of the solution. The MRS team's idea was simple: leverage complementary capabilities of different vendors and sources to create a unified database that is best suited to deal with these challenges of malicious and inappropriate material. This made it possible to implement a scalable architecture that allows multiple streams of data to be incorporated into a merged database. This way, each vendor and source brings its unique strengths to a common solution.

The URL category information obtained from MRS is used at different places in Forefront TMG:

- **Firewall rules**   The firewall administrator allows or denies access according to the category.
- **Web proxy log**   The category is written in the log for each request (and will be used for reporting).
- **Malware inspection exclusion list**   A list of URLs that shouldn't be inspected by the malware filter is maintained.
- **HTTPS exclusion list**   A list of URLs that you don't want to inspect (those belonging to the Financial category, for example) is maintained.

The URL Filtering feature can be enabled in three different places on the Forefront TMG Management console: the Getting Started Wizard, the Web Access Policy option, and the Web Access Policy Wizard. After enabling URL filtering, the Enable URL Filtering option appears, as shown in Figure 1-8.

> **NOTE**   For more information on how to configure URL Filtering on Forefront TMG, read Chapter 18, "URL Filtering," in *Microsoft Forefront Threat Management Gateway (TMG) Administrator's Companion*, from Microsoft Press.

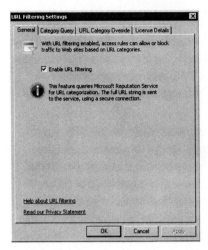

FIGURE 1-8

Improvements to the URL filtering database coverage and accuracy are made on an ongoing basis. In order to further improve data quality, a URL filtering telemetry mechanism was developed and built into the product. This mechanism allows the MRS team to review URL filtering data samples collected from participating Forefront TMG deployments. Based on those samples, the MRS team can analyze URL filtering coverage and accuracy, identify pain points, and address those pain points accordingly. This mechanism is critical for ensuring a quality URL filtering service that addresses the kind of Web traffic that is seen in customers' businesses.

Forefront TMG Role within the Forefront Protection Suite

Forefront TMG is just one of a number of security-specific applications that populate the Forefront Protection Suite. Forefront includes security applications in four main areas:

- **Forefront Edge security applications**   Forefront edge security solutions include Forefront TMG and Forefront Unified Access Gateway (UAG) 2010.

- **Forefront Server security applications**   These include Microsoft Forefront Protection for Exchange Server (FPE) and Microsoft Forefront Protection for SharePoint (FPSP). In addition, there is Microsoft Forefront Online Protection for Exchange (FOPE), which provides a cloud-based Exchange security solution.

- **Forefront host security application**   This group currently includes Microsoft Forefront Endpoint Protection (FEP).

- **Forefront identity security application**   This includes Microsoft Forefront Identity Manager (FIM), which enables self-service capabilities for users to create entities, such as groups. In addition, it allows streamlined management of certificates and provides integration services for multiple authentication repositories, enabling centralized account management.

> **NOTE** For more information, refer to the following two titles from Microsoft Press:
> - *Deploying Microsoft Forefront Protection 2010 for Exchange Server*
> - *Deploying Microsoft Forefront Unified Access Gateway 2010*

Let's take a look at some of the products that are part of the Forefront Protection Suite.

Forefront Unified Access Gateway 2010

The Microsoft Forefront Unified Access Gateway (UAG) 2010 represents the latest version of the original Microsoft Intelligent Application Gateway (IAG) 2007. UAG is designed to provide a comprehensive and unified solution for remote access into the corporate network by enabling multiple remote access technologies in a single server solution. However, UAG provides more than remote access; UAG helps you to *secure* remote access in a number of remote access scenarios.

UAG employs multiple remote access technologies because different users will require different types of access. For example, a non-domain computer might need administrative, network level access to much of the corporate network, so you could provide SSTP VPN access to that user. Another user might need access to desktop applications and data from remote locations, so you could give that user RDP access over Terminal Services Gateway (TSG). Other users might only need access to key Web applications, such as OWA or SharePoint. In that case, you could publish these sites using secure reverse proxy. Finally, domain member computers outside the network might need full corporate network access that is exactly the same as the end-user experience when the user is directly connected to the corporate network over a wired or wireless connection. In this case, you could provide DirectAccess. You can use UAG to support all these remote access scenarios and more.

Some of the key features and capabilities available in UAG include:

- Secure Web application publishing with application layer firewall, including positive and negative logic filters.
- Integrated Terminal Services Gateway to publish remote desktops.
- Integrated Terminal Services Gateway to publish RemoteApps.
- Client/server publishing to support secure remote access to non-Web applications.
- Network layer SSTP VPN server for full network-level access over traditional VPN connections.
- File server publishing, enabling remote access to corporate network file servers.
- DirectAccess, a new way to provide native on-network connectivity to managed remote access clients, enabling a full on-network experience to remote access users anywhere in the world.

- Comprehensive support for multiple authentication repositories and authentication methods, including many types of two-factor authentication.

- Endpoint detection and control, enabling policies to be set so that client access is based on both who the user is and the state of the machine from which the user connects; this also provides customized access to resources depending on the nature or state of the connecting computer.

- Log-on portal that provides a simple portal experience for end users to select the applications which they are authorized to use. The user needs to remember only one URL to access Web and non-Web applications, as well as VPN connections, if they are required.

To protect itself and any networks behind UAG, Forefront TMG is installed on the UAG server. Because Forefront TMG is installed on the UAG server, it is designed to be an edge device and can be placed at the edge of an enterprise network. However, like Forefront TMG, UAG is flexible and can be placed at any one of a number of perimeters within the network.

Administrator Insight

Although TMG is installed when you install UAG, TMG is only configured through the UAG Management console. TMG is designed to protect the UAG server and prevent attackers from reaching networks behind the UAG server. The TMG server installed on the UAG server cannot be used for any outbound access controls and cannot be used for scenarios that are not supported by UAG.

Forefront Identity Manager

Forefront Identity Manager (FIM) changes the current state of identity management by providing powerful end user self-service capabilities. IT professionals are also given more tools to solve day-to-day tasks, such as delegating administration and creating workflows for common identity management tasks. In addition, FIM is built on a .NET- and WS-* based foundation so that developers can build more customized and extensible solutions.

- Allows end users to perform self-service tasks, such as creating distribution lists.

- Provides a development environment to manage identities through SharePoint and workflow management consoles.

- Integrates identities that are stored in various repositories, directories, and databases.

- Enables centralized management of distributed identities.

- Enables streamlining of certificate management.

- Enables integrated auditing and compliance.

FIM 2010 is primarily concerned with identity management and less with network, host, and service security. For this reason, this book does not cover FIM and does not describe the relationships between FIM and other Forefront products.

Forefront Protection for Exchange Server

Forefront Protection for Exchange Server (FPE) is an antivirus/anti-malware and spam filtering solution for Microsoft Exchange environments. FPE can be deployed in a number of ways. First, FPE can be installed on the Edge Server so that it can inspect email moving into and out of the corporate network. Second, FPE can be deployed on an Exchange Hub Transport Server so that email can be inspected as it moves within the organization. Finally, FPE can be installed on the mailbox server, so that it can inspect the contents of user mailboxes and provide real time protection against malicious attachments.

FPE is part of the two-member family of Forefront server protection products. The other product in this family is Forefront Protection for SharePoint, which performs similar duties to protect SharePoint sites.

Forefront Protection for Exchange Server includes:

- Malware protection with a multi-engine scanner.
- Premium anti-spam capabilities.
- The ability to block unwanted or dangerous attachments.
- The ability to prevent data theft.
- One-click provisioning for hosted services.
- A comprehensive messaging security dashboard.
- Automatic signature update capability.

FPE is automatically installed on the Forefront TMG firewall whenever the secure email gateway role is enabled. This allows Forefront TMG to work with the back-end components of FPE to provide multiple levels of protection for your email organization.

Forefront Online Protection for Exchange

Microsoft Forefront Online Protection for Exchange (FOPE) is a cloud-based solution that provides edge email protection and services similar to the services enabled by the Exchange Edge Server role. However, it is important to note that FOPE does not provide the same feature set as that provided by either Exchange Edge or Forefront Protection for Exchange.

FOPE includes:

- Anti-malware scanning for both inbound and outbound email.
- Spam detection for both inbound and outbound email.
- Policy enforcement on both inbound and outbound email.

The policy enforcement feature is unique for FOPE. Policy enforcement allows you to create policies to perform tasks such as encrypting email before forwarding it to its destination.

For example, suppose your company does business with a high security agency of the government and the agency requires that all mail that is addressed to it must be encrypted. You can use FOPE policies to enforce email encryption for any mail addressed to that destination. Users do not need to be aware of this policy, because the policy enforcement and encryption takes place in the cloud. The email is encrypted from end to end, because the link between your site and the FOPE cloud datacenter is encrypted with SMTPS.

FOPE can also be configured to work with your current on-premises Exchange Server solution. Forefront Protection for Exchange currently supports integrated provisioning and management of FOPE, enabling a hybrid on-premises and cloud solution for email protection.

Forefront Protection 2010 for SharePoint

Forefront Protection 2010 for SharePoint (FPSP) is an anti-malware and content inspection system used to protect SharePoint Server sites from malware and inappropriate content. FPSP is installed on the SharePoint Servers themselves and is configured in the SharePoint Management console.

Key features included in Forefront Protection for SharePoint include:

- Multiple antivirus engines.
- Protection against inappropriate content.
- Document filtering.
- Protection against new and hidden threats.
- Multi-vendor response to new threats.
- Out-of-policy file blocking.
- Performance control settings.
- A Web-based management interface for enterprise deployments.

FPE works together with FSE, FEP, and Forefront TMG to make sure that clients, servers, and gateways all work together to protect the network against malicious software and inappropriate content.

Administrators Punch List

Key takeaways from this chapter:

- Unlike Proxy Server, ISA and TMG are designed to be edge network-level firewalls.
- TMG does not trust any network. All networks are subject to stateful packet and application layer inspection.
- The improvements over ISA 2006 features that are included in TMG are focused on outbound access control. The only improvement for remote access is the new support for SSTP.

- Typical TMG placement scenarios include front-end firewall, back-end firewall, and single-NIC web proxy server.

- TMG can act as a network firewall, forward and reverse web proxy server, forward Winsock proxy server, remote outbound SSL bridging access VPN server, and site-to-site VPN gateway.

- TMG includes new Web anti-malware and URL filtering that provides protection for forward proxy scenarios.

- TMG adds support for outbound SSL bridging, which enables TMG to inspect the contents of SSL connections in a forward proxy scenario; TMG also support inbound SSL briding, so that it can inspect contents of connections in reverse proxy (Web publishing) scenarios.

- The TMG VPN server and site-to-site VPN gateway configuration enforce the same stateful packet and application layer inspection as any other connection to or through the TMG firewall.

- The TMG firewall can act as secure email gateway when the Exchange Edge Server role is installed on the firewall. Unlike non-TMG scenarios, the TMG firewall hosting the Exchange Edge Server role can be a domain member, and this is generally the recommended configuration.

- New to TMG is the Network Inspection System (NIS), which is designed to be an IDS/IPS with a primary focus on Microsoft-related security issues.

CHAPTER 2

Installing and Configuring Forefront Threat Management Gateway 2010

Forefront TMG is a multifunction device that can fill many roles in protecting your network. Forefront TMG can act as a network firewall, remote access VPN server, site-to-site VPN gateway, Web access protection device (using Web anti-malware, HTTPS inspection, and URL filtering), forward and reverse proxy, and network Intrusion Detection System/Intrusion Prevention System (IDP/IPS) device. In addition to determining the role that your Forefront TMG firewall will play on your network, you'll need to do some preparation in advance. That preparation will help ensure that Forefront TMG is best able to perform the duties you intend for it.

This chapter provides a discussion about preparing for installing Forefront TMG and then goes through the actual steps required to install Forefront TMG in your environment.

Preparing to Install Forefront TMG

While there are many things to consider prior to installing a Forefront TMG solution on your network, there are three primary areas that deserve special attention. These three areas are:

- Choosing the right Forefront TMG deployment option for your environment

- Meeting hardware and software requirements for your selected deployment option

- Selecting the right Forefront TMG edition for your deployment

After these core planning decisions are made, you will be ready to begin installing your stand-alone Forefront TMG firewall or Forefront TMG array.

Choosing Deployment Options for Forefront TMG

Before you selected Forefront TMG as your solution, you had certain requirements that needed to be met. That is to say, you had a problem that needed to be solved, and you determined that Forefront TMG was the right solution for your problem. Now is the right time to revisit the problem you were seeking to solve with Forefront TMG so that you can choose the correct deployment options to fit your needs.

Forefront TMG can fill multiple roles in your organization's network infrastructure. When planning roles for your Forefront TMG deployment, determining the appropriate number of network interface cards (NICs) required by the solution is critical because not all of the solutions are supported by a single-NIC configuration. However, the single-NIC configuration is popular because the application owner doesn't need to bring in the network team. Aside from this consideration, all the roles are interoperable, meaning that you can configure your Forefront TMG firewall to support multiple roles on a single computer or on a single array of Forefront TMG firewalls or Web proxies.

The Forefront TMG roles include:

- **Network Firewall** In its role as a network firewall, Forefront TMG can be placed on the edge of the corporate network to help protect your network from external attack, prevent users on the corporate network from attacking other networks, and control the sites and protocols that users can access when connecting to the Internet. As a network firewall, Forefront TMG will need at least two network interfaces.

- **Forward and Reverse Proxy** In its role as a forward and reverse proxy, Forefront TMG can handle both inbound and outbound HTTP/HTTPS traffic. Forefront TMG can act as a forward or reverse proxy solution with one or more NICs, but a single-NIC solution significantly reduces the number of deployment scenarios that Forefront TMG will support.

- **Forward Winsock Proxy** In its role as a forward Winsock proxy server, Forefront TMG can provide added security when Winsock-based network applications try to connect to the Internet. Network calls by Winsock applications are intercepted by the Forefront TMG client and forwarded directly to the Forefront TMG firewall. This reduces the number of routing issues on your network. In addition, as a Winsock proxy solution, Forefront TMG is able to track and record the names of the applications users use to connect to the Internet, the name of each user who uses each application, and the name of each computer from which each application was accessed. Forefront TMG must have two or more NICs to support the Winsock proxy solution.

- **Remote Access VPN Server** The remote access VPN server role allows users to establish PPTP, L2TP/IPsec, or SSTP connections to the Forefront TMG VPN server to connect to resources on the corporate network. The remote access VPN server role can be deployed on computers with one or more NICs.

- **Site-to-Site VPN Gateway** In its role as a site-to-site VPN gateway, Forefront TMG can connect two or more networks over the Internet using PPTP, L2TP/IPsec or IPsec tunnel mode. The preferred method, from both a security and a performance perspective, is L2TP/IPsec. However, if you need to connect your Forefront TMG site-to-site VPN gateway to non-Forefront TMG /ISA VPN gateways, you will need to use IPsec tunnel mode. PPTP should be avoided because it provides the lowest security levels, but some of the security concerns regarding PPTP can be mitigated by using EAP authentication.

- **Web Access Protection** Web access protection is a subset of the Forefront TMG firewall's forward proxy capabilities. You can deploy a Forefront TMG solution with one or more NICs to help prevent security incidents using Forefront TMG's Web anti-malware and URL filtering capabilities.

- **Network Intrusion Detection System/Intrusion Prevention System (IDS/IPS)** Forefront TMG includes a new feature, called the Network Inspection System (NIS), that enables all traffic moving to and through the firewall to be inspected for exploits targeted against Microsoft assets. Signatures for NIS are updated frequently to help increase the security delivered by NIS.

- **Email Protection Gateway** A new role introduced with Forefront TMG is the email protection gateway feature set. You can use Forefront TMG as your edge email protection solution. Forefront TMG takes advantage of the Exchange Edge Server role and also supports Forefront Protection for Exchange to provide a defense in depth anti-spam and anti-malware solution for protecting your email organization. While it was designed to provide enhanced protection for Microsoft Exchange, Forefront TMG can also be used as an edge email protection solution for any SMTP-based solution you currently use.

 SECURITY ALERT A single-NIC TMG firewall supports only forward and reverse Web proxy roles. If you require support for protocols other than HTTP/HTTPS, the TMG firewall must be configured as a multi-homed device. The single-NIC TMG firewall provides far fewer security options than a multi-homed TMG firewall provides.

Meeting Hardware and Software Requirements for Forefront TMG

You must meet at least the minimum hardware requirements for Forefront TMG, but in almost all cases, you will want to exceed those requirements. Table 2-1 lists the minimum hardware requirements and the recommended hardware requirements for computers that will host the Forefront TMG firewall services. Table 2-2 lists the minimum software requirements. Tables 2-3 and 2-4 list the requirements for the Enterprise Management Server role.

TABLE 2-1 Hardware Requirements for Forefront TMG

HARDWARE	REQUIREMENTS	RECOMMENDATIONS
CPU	Intel or AMD Processor 64-bit-capable Dual core	Intel or AMD Processor Quad core or two dual core Hyper-threading-capable
RAM	2 GB 1 GHz RAM	4 GB 1 GHz RAM
Hard Drive	2.5 GB for Forefront TMG software Additional required for: Web caching Malware inspection caching Logging NTFS-formatted	Additional for: Web content caching Logging
Network Interfaces	At least one NIC (Single-NIC configuration limits the number of roles that can be supported)	Two or more NICs Additional NICs can be configured as external, perimeter or internal networks

TABLE 2-2 Software Requirements for Forefront TMG

SOFTWARE	REQUIREMENTS
Operating system	Windows Server 2008 or Windows Server 2008 R2 Editions supported: ■ Standard ■ Enterprise ■ Datacenter

Windows Server roles and features	Server roles and features required by Forefront TMG include:
	▪ Network Policy Server
	▪ Routing and Remote Access Service
	▪ Active Directory Lightweight Directory Services
	▪ Network Load Balancing
	▪ Windows PowerShell
	These server roles are installed during Forefront TMG installation; you do not need to install them in advance. However, they are not removed if you uninstall Forefront TMG. If you need to remove these roles later, you must do so manually.
Other software	During installation, the Forefront TMG Preparation Tool also installs the following features:
	▪ Microsoft .NET Framework 3.5 SP1
	▪ Windows Web Services API
	▪ Microsoft Update
	▪ Microsoft Windows Installer 4.5

NOTE Forefront TMG is not supported on a machine that is configured as a domain controller, with the exception of a read-only domain controller, which requires that TMG Service Pack 1 be installed.

Requirements for Enterprise Management Server

If you worked with ISA Server 2004 or ISA Server 2006, you might recall that ISA Server Standard Edition stored firewall policy and configuration in the local Registry, while the Enterprise Edition of the ISA firewall stored firewall policy and configuration in the Active Directory Application Mode (ADAM) database. This difference between Standard and Enterprise Editions is not the case in Forefront TMG.

Both the Standard and Enterprise editions of Forefront TMG store their configurations in an Active Directory Lightweight Directories Services (AD LDS) database. For the Standard Edition, the AD LDS database is always on the Forefront TMG firewall itself. With the Enterprise Edition, you have the option of installing the AD LDS configuration database on a firewall array member or on a separate computer. The separate computer hosting the AD LDS database is called the Enterprise Management Server (EMS). The EMS performs a role similar to that performed by the Configuration Storage Server used by ISA Server 2004 and ISA Server 2006. Table 2-3 shows the hardware requirements for the Enterprise Management Server.

TABLE 2-3 Hardware Requirements for the Enterprise Management Server

HARDWARE	REQUIREMENTS
CPU	Intel or AMD Processor 64-bit-capable Dual core
RAM	1 GB
Hard Drive	2.5 GB for the EMS software Formatted as NTFS

TABLE 2-4 Software Requirements for the Enterprise Management Server

SOFTWARE	HARDWARE
Operating System	Windows Server 2008 or Windows Server 2008 R2 Editions supported: ■ Standard ■ Enterprise ■ Datacenter
Windows roles and features	Active Directory Lightweight Directory Services
Other software	Other software installed on the server to support the EMS role: ■ Microsoft.NET Framework 3.5 SP1 ■ Microsoft Windows Installer 4.5

Requirements for the Forefront TMG Remote Console

There are multiple ways in which you can manage your Forefront TMG firewall or Forefront TMG firewall array.

- One option is to go to the data center and sit in front of the console. You would only want to do this in the most dire circumstances because, in most cases, the data center will be quite a distance from where you work.

- A better option might be to use Remote Desktop to remotely connect to your firewall or firewall array. This option provides you with access to the desktop interface so that you can manage both the Forefront TMG firewall components and any operating system components that might need configuration.

- A third option is to use a remote Forefront TMG console. The remote Forefront TMG console allows you to manage the Forefront TMG firewall components that are exposed in the Forefront TMG firewall console. However, there are some limitations in this approach, including the fact that changes made from a remote console are not saved in the change management log, and you do not have access to the components of the operating system that lie outside the Forefront TMG console's interface but that you might need to configure in order to manage the firewall or firewall array.

Table 2-5 lists the hardware requirements and Table 2-6 lists the software requirements for installing the Forefront TMG remote console on a workstation or server.

TABLE 2-5 Hardware Requirements for the Forefront TMG Remote Console

HARDWARE	REQUIREMENTS
CPU	1 GHz processor
RAM	1 GB RAM
Hard Drive	2 GB of space for the management console software NTFS-formatted volume

TABLE 2-6 Software Requirements for the Forefront TMG Remote Console

SOFTWARE	REQUIREMENTS
Operating System	One of the following: ■ Windows Server 2008 ■ Windows Server 2008 R2 ■ Windows 7 ■ Windows Vista SP1 Both 32-bit and 64-bit versions of the Forefront TMG management console are available.

Selecting the Forefront TMG Edition

Another important decision you will need to make prior to installing Forefront TMG is which edition best fits your needs. As in ISA Server, there are two editions: Standard Edition and Enterprise Edition. Forefront TMG Standard Edition is similar to the ISA Server Standard Edition in that it supports a single-server configuration and there is no array, Network Load Balancing (NLB), Cache Array Routing Protocol (CARP), or off-box configuration support. In contrast, Forefront TMG Enterprise Edition supports, as ISA Server Enterprise Edition did, enterprise array configuration, NLB, CARP and off-box configuration support, using the Enterprise Management Server.

Table 2-7 provides a side-by-side comparison of Forefront TMG Standard and Enterprise Editions to help you decide which edition best meets your organizational requirements.

TABLE 2-7 Forefront TMG Standard Edition and Enterprise Edition Comparison

DESCRIPTION	STANDARD EDITION	ENTERPRISE EDITION
Deployment scenarios	Stand-alone server No array support	Stand-alone array (Forefront TMG array without Enterprise Management Server) Enterprise Management Server managed array
CPU	Up to 4 CPU Sockets	Unlimited
Storage	Local No support for off-box configuration storage	Local Off-box with Enterprise Management Server
Enterprise array	No	Yes
Network Load Balancing (NLB)	No	Yes – support for both uni-cast and multicast modes
Cache Array Routing Protocol (CARP)	No	Yes – support for both client- and server-side CARP
Enterprise Management Server	No	Yes – Enterprise Management Server can manage both enterprise arrays and stand-alone Standard Edition firewalls
Web and server publishing	Yes	Yes
Remote access VPN server	Yes	Yes
Site-to-site VPN gateway	Yes	Yes
Forward proxy	Yes	Yes
Forward and reverse caching	Yes	Yes
Network Inspection System (IDS/IPS)	Yes	Yes
Email protection	Yes – Requires Exchange license for Exchange Edge Server Role	Yes – Requires Exchange license for Exchange Edge Server role
Web anti-malware and URL filtering	Yes – requires user licensing	Yes – requires user licensing

Installing Forefront TMG

After you review all the Forefront TMG hardware and software requirements and plan your deployment, you're ready to install the product. As with any product installation, it is important to review these requirements before you start the installation process. This section describes how to install Forefront TMG, using the fictitious Contoso Ltd. as an example where specific company information is required.

Reviewing Company Requirements

Many company requirements are identified during the planning phase; however, we all know that sometimes (mostly because there are time constraints) this phase is skipped, and a checklist is created right before the installation takes place. You should plan sufficient time to analyze your requirements and document them carefully. Then you can create a meaningful installation checklist. This installation checklist should have at least three core sections:

- **Network Topology** It is important to understand where within the network's topology Forefront TMG will be placed. To better understand this you will need at least a simplified version of the company's network diagram.

- **Installation Location** It is important to identify the drive on which Forefront TMG will be installed.

- **Main Post-Installation steps** It is important to know what needs to be configured first in order to allow the company to use Forefront TMG in production after it is installed.

The scenario used for this example is based on the simplified topology shown in Figure 2-1:

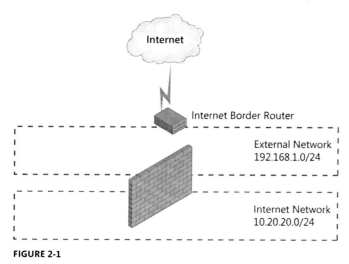

FIGURE 2-1

In this scenario, Forefront TMG has two network interfaces: one connected to the external network with the address 192.168.1.0/24 and the other connected to the internal network with the address 10.20.20.0/24. The initial requirements for Forefront TMG for the Contoso network are:

- Allow all authenticated users to access the Internet, but only for HTTP and HTTPS traffic
- Block access to some Web destinations based on the type of site
- Perform malware inspection
- Perform outbound HTTPS inspection
- Do not notify users that the traffic is being inspected
- Have 1 GB of Web cache
- Do not create additional services within the internal network (for example, there is no internal CA and a new one cannot be installed)

These requirements for Forefront TMG for the Contoso network will be implemented in the post-installation phase.

NOTE Before you install Forefront TMG, it is recommended that you rename the network interfaces in Windows to names that reflect the location of the adapters, for example, Internal and External adapters. This will facilitate network identification, not only during Forefront TMG setup, but also in other situations.

Completing the Installation Phases

The Forefront TMG installation requires that you complete three tasks:

- Ensure that the operating system is up to date by running Windows Update before installing Forefront TMG.
- Prepare the Windows operating system to install Forefront TMG. The TMG installer will check that required components are installed and will automatically install those that are missing from the operating system.
- Install Forefront TMG and select the appropriate options for your environment.

Installing Forefront TMG

Put the Forefront TMG DVD into the server's DVD drive and complete the following steps to start the installation.

NOTE The installation steps used here assume you are installing the Forefront TMG Enterprise Edition. Installation steps are similar for the Standard Edition, and the following steps provide enough information so that you will be able to understand the Standard Edition installation routine.

1. The Windows operating system reads the DVD content and starts the installation based on the autorun parameters. A splash screen similar to the one in Figure 2-2 will appear. If autorun is disabled, open and execute the file **autorun.hta**, and the splash screen should appear.

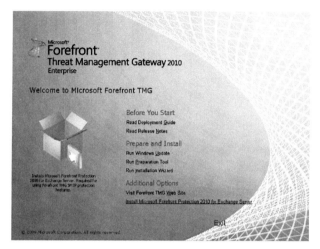

FIGURE 2-2

2. Assuming that you ran Windows Update prior to running Forefront TMG setup, click the option Run Preparation Tool. The Welcome To The Preparation Tool For Microsoft Forefront Threat Management Gateway (TMG) page appears, as shown in Figure 2-3.

FIGURE 2-3

3. Click Next to proceed, and then read the License Agreement page. After reading it, make sure to select the I Accept The Terms Of The License Agreements checkbox, as shown in Figure 2-4. Click Next to proceed.

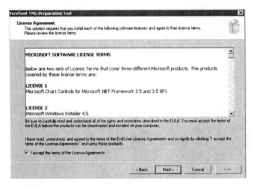

FIGURE 2-4

4. The Installation Type page, shown in Figure 2-5, allows you to select the Forefront TMG components that you want to install.

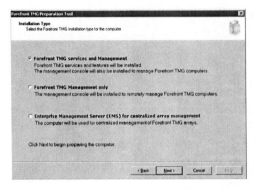

FIGURE 2-5

Select one of the following options, and then click Next.

- **Forefront TMG Services And Management**   This option is the default. Use this option to install all Forefront TMG services, including Firewall and Configuration Store and the Forefront TMG Management console.

- **Forefront TMG Management Only**   Use this option when you want to install only the Forefront TMG console. This option is usually used by Firewall administrators who want to manage Forefront TMG remotely (from a workstation, for instance).

- **Enterprise Management Server (EMS) For Centralized Array Management**   Choose this option if you want to install only the EMS role that will allow you to manage multiple Forefront TMG arrays from a single location.

5. The Forefront TMG Preparation Tool starts to review the system and, based on your selections, it will verify that the components that need to be in place before the Forefront TMG installation starts are in place. This process can take some time, and while this is taking place a new page with a progress bar appears, as shown in Figure 2-6.

FIGURE 2-6

6. When the process finishes, the Preparation Complete page, shown in Figure 2-7, appears. Notice that the Launch Forefront TMG Installation Wizard checkbox is selected by default. If you don't have time to continue the setup now, you can clear the checkbox and proceed later, knowing that the operating system is already prepared to install TMG. In this case, leave the checkbox selected, and then click Finish to continue.

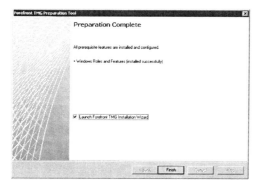

FIGURE 2-7

7. The first thing that will happen when the preparation tool finishes is that a Microsoft Forefront TMG Installation Wizard progress page appears. It lists three phases, as shown in Figure 2-8. An arrow pointer to the left of the phase identifies the phase that is in progress. Each phase description includes an estimate of the time required to complete the setup.

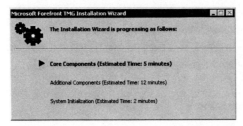

FIGURE 2-8

8. The progress page will remain open throughout the entire setup, and another page will pop up to display the Installation Wizard. The first page that appears is the Welcome To The Installation Wizard For Forefront TMG Enterprise, shown in Figure 2-9. Click Next to proceed.

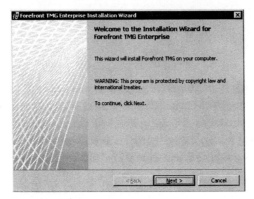

FIGURE 2-9

9. Read the License Agreement page, and then select the I Accept The Terms In The License Agreement option, as shown in Figure 2-10. Click Next to proceed.

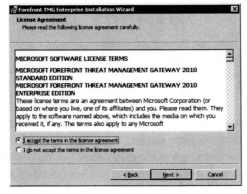

FIGURE 2-10

10. Type the information required to identify your software license: User Name, Organization, and the Product Serial Number, as shown in Figure 2-11. Click Next to continue.

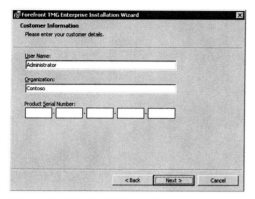

FIGURE 2-11

11. On the Installation Path page, you identify the location in which Forefront TMG will be installed. If during the planning phase you decided that Forefront TMG will be located in a different partition (or disk) and will not be installed on the same drive as the operating system, this is your chance to change it. Once this process is complete, you can only change the installation location by uninstalling Forefront TMG and installing it again. Select the location shown in Figure 2-12, and then click Next to display the Define Internal Network page.

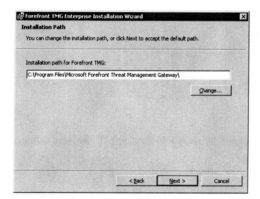

FIGURE 2-12

12. The Define Internal Network page requires you to specify which network interface is considered to be internal (connected to your corporate network). Click Add, and the Addresses dialog box, shown in Figure 2-13, appears.

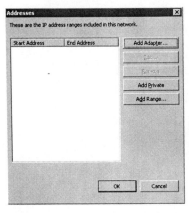

FIGURE 2-13

13. Click Add Adapter, and then select the Network Adapter that will be used to communicate with the internal network, as shown in Figure 2-14. Click OK to continue.

FIGURE 2-14

14. The Addresses dialog box appears again, as shown in Figure 2-15. Review the address range, and then click OK to confirm.

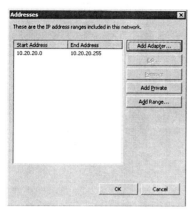

FIGURE 2-15

15. On the Define Internal Network page, shown in Figure 2-16, you will see that the range now reflects the start and end addresses of the Contoso network. Click Next to continue.

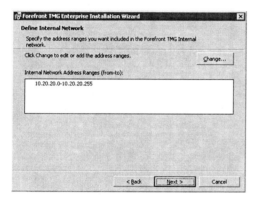

FIGURE 2-16

16. The Services Warning page, shown in Figure 2-17, warns you that some services will be restarted during this process and that Routing and Remote Access Service (RRAS) will be stopped. Click Next to proceed.

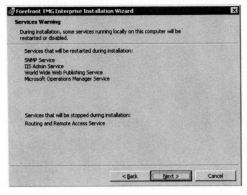

FIGURE 2-17

17. The Ready To Install The Program page, shown in Figure 2-18, is the final page before the setup starts to make changes in the system. Click Install to continue.

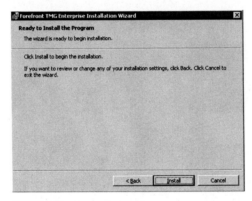

FIGURE 2-18

18. During this phase, many changes will be made in the system, and the progress page will identify the correct status as the process advances, as shown in Figures 2-19 and 2-20.

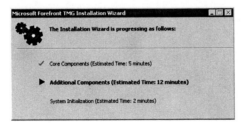

FIGURE 2-19

FIGURE 2-20

19. When the last phase successfully finishes, you will see the Installation Wizard Completed page, shown in Figure 2-21. Click Finish to conclude the installation process.

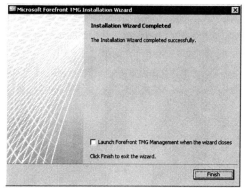

FIGURE 2-21

20. After this page closes, Internet Explorer will open and display a Protect The Forefront TMG Server page, shown in Figure 2-22. This page describes some additional security recommendations.

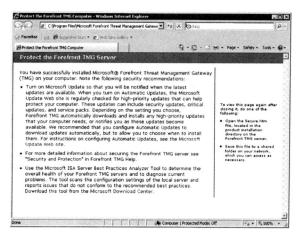

FIGURE 2-22

The installation is finished, and now it is necessary to properly configure Forefront TMG to adjust to the environment's needs.

Post-Installation Configuration

After installing Forefront TMG, you need to complete the post-installation and configuration tasks. Immediately following installation, there is only one rule (Deny All) in place, and it denies all requests. This rule is designed to block everything because no requests were identified as being safe to open. However, when you open the Forefront TMG Management console for the first time, the Getting Started Wizard opens to guide you through the initial setup.

This wizard allows you to configure network settings, system settings, and initial deployment options. After finishing those three tasks, this wizard invokes another wizard that allows you to create a Web access policy and specify the traffic that you want to allow. Take the following steps to complete the post-installation configuration:

1. Click Start, All Programs, Microsoft Forefront TMG, and then click Forefront TMG Management to open the TMG console. The first page that appears is the Getting Started Wizard, shown in Figure 2-23.

FIGURE 2-23

2. Click Configure Network Settings and the Welcome To The Network Setup Wizard page appears, as shown in Figure 2-24. Click Next to continue.

FIGURE 2-24

3. On the Network Template Selection page, shown in Figure 2-25, you select the network template that Forefront TMG will use. In this case, Edge Firewall is the most appropriate option because TMG has one interface connected to the internal network and another connected to the external network. Notice in Figure 2-25 that the 3-Leg Perimeter option is not available. The reason is that this Forefront TMG installation has only two network interface cards, so it is not possible to use this template. Leave the Edge Firewall template selected, and then click Next to proceed.

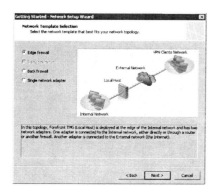

FIGURE 2-25

4. On the Local Area Network (LAN) Settings page, click the drop-down arrow for the Network Adapter Connected To The LAN option and select the NIC that is connected to the internal network (in this example, the NIC has been renamed "Internal"), as shown in Figure 2-26. The IP address settings from the interface card that is connected to the internal network will appear. If you have multiple networks behind the internal network, you can add the IP address range for that network. For example, in this case, the internal network is 10.20.20.0/24; if the internal network is also connected to another network, such as 10.30.30.0/24, you can add this range. Then you can specify which gateway to use to reach that network by clicking the Add button in the Specify

Additional Network Topology Routes (Optional) section. Complete the information, and then click Next to continue.

FIGURE 2-26

5. The Internet Settings page is similar to the LAN Settings page. This page should already display the address, mask, gateway, and DNS information, as shown in Figure 2-27. Verify that there is a default gateway defined and that there is no DNS setting specified (because it is on the internal interface). Click Next to proceed.

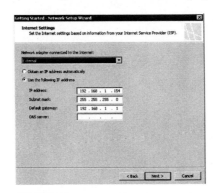

FIGURE 2-27

> **NOTE** For best practices in configuring DNS settings on Forefront TMG, read "Planning for DNS Name Resolution" at *http://technet.microsoft.com/en-us/library /cc995245.aspx.*

6. On the Completing The Network Setup Wizard page, click Finish to conclude the first step of the Getting Started Wizard. The Getting Started Wizard Welcome page will appear, as shown in Figure 2-28. Click Configure System Settings to proceed.

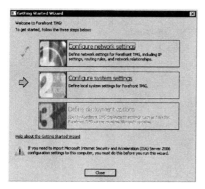

FIGURE 2-28

7. The Welcome To The System Configuration Wizard page appears, as shown in Figure 2-29. Click Next to continue.

FIGURE 2-29

8. On the Host Identification page, you can change the computer name and the domain membership, as shown in Figure 2-30. Either leave the default or enter your changes, click Next, and then click Finish to conclude the second part of the Getting Started Wizard.

FIGURE 2-30

9. The third and last step of the Getting Started Wizard is now available, as shown in Figure 2-31. Click Define Deployment Options to continue.

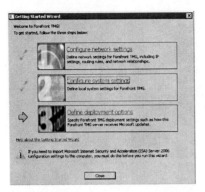

FIGURE 2-31

10. The Welcome To The Deployment Wizard page appears, as shown in Figure 2-32. Click Next to continue.

FIGURE 2-32

11. The Microsoft Update Setup page allows you to configure the way Forefront TMG will be updated. It is recommended that you leave the Use The Microsoft Update Service To Check For Updates (Recommended) option selected, as shown in Figure 2-33. Click Next to proceed.

FIGURE 2-33

12. On the Forefront TMG Protection Features Settings page, you activate the free Network Inspection System (NIS) license and the evaluation license for Web Protection. Enable Malware Inspection is selected by default, as shown in Figure 2-34. Make your selections, and then click Next to continue.

FIGURE 2-34

> **NOTE** For more information on the license for Web Protection, review "Pricing and Licensing" at *http://www.microsoft.com/forefront/threat-management-gateway/en/us /pricing-licensing.aspx.*

13. On the NIS Signature Update Settings page, shown in Figure 2-35, you can configure the way Forefront TMG will check and install new definitions. By default, the timing for automatic polling is set to 15 minutes, and it will trigger an alert after 45 days if updates were not installed. Make your selections, and then click Next to continue.

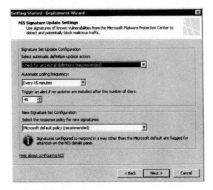

FIGURE 2-35

14. On the Customer Feedback page there are two options. The option to participate in the Customer Experience Improvement Program is selected by default, as shown in Figure 2-36. Make your selection, and then click Next to continue.

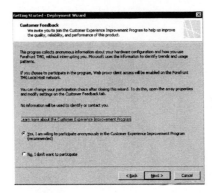

FIGURE 2-36

15. On the Microsoft Telemetry Reporting Service page, shown in Figure 2-37, you can select your level of participation in this service. This reporting service is designed to help Microsoft identify attack patterns and mitigate threats. Review the options that are available, and make the selection that adheres to your company policies and is best for your environment. Click Next to proceed.

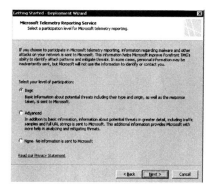

FIGURE 2-37

16. Once all three steps of the Getting Started Wizard have been finished, review your selections, and then click Finish. The Run The Web Access Wizard option is enabled by default. When you click Close, the Web Access Policy Wizard, shown in Figure 2-38, will start. Click Next to continue.

FIGURE 2-38

17. The first option in the Web Access Policy Wizard is about rule creation, as shown in Figure 2-39. In the deployment planning phase, the Contoso Company determined that they will need an access rule that allows HTTP and HTTPS but blocks a pre-selected number of Web site categories, so leave the default option enabled, and then click Next to continue.

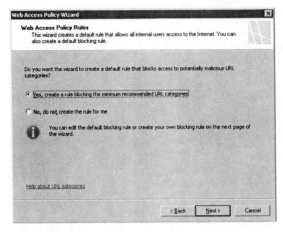

FIGURE 2-39

18. The Blocked Web Destination page lists recommended categories of URLs that should be blocked, as shown in Figure 2-40. Those categories will be used by the URL Filtering Feature. For this exercise, leave the default options enabled, and then click Next to continue.

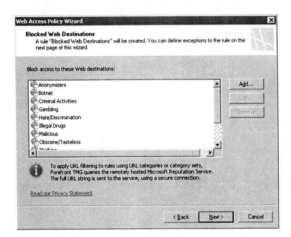

FIGURE 2-40

> **NOTE** For more information on URL Filtering configuration, read Chapter 18, "URL Filtering," in *Microsoft Forefront Threat Management Gateway (TMG) Administrator's Companion*, from Microsoft Press.

19. On the Blocked Web Destination Exceptions page, shown in Figure 2-41, you can add users or groups that will have unrestricted access to the Web. For Contoso's require-

ments, no user will have unrestricted Web access, so leave this list blank, and then click Next to continue.

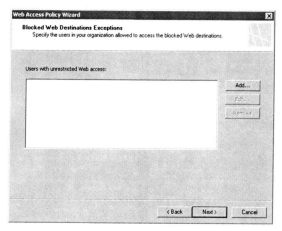

FIGURE 2-41

20. On the Malware Inspection Settings page, shown in Figure 2-42, you choose whether to enable malware inspection for outbound traffic. By default, the Web Access Policy Wizard enables this feature and also blocks encrypted archive files. Contoso wants malware inspection to be enabled in the edge, so leave the default options enabled, and then click Next to proceed.

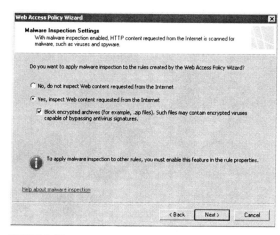

FIGURE 2-42

NOTE For more information on Malware Inspection configuration, read Chapter 17, "Malware Inspection," in *Microsoft Forefront Threat Management Gateway (TMG) Administrator's Companion*, from Microsoft Press.

21. The HTTPS Inspection Settings page, shown in Figure 2-43, allows you to define the way Forefront TMG should handle HTTPS traffic. By default, the option to inspect HTTPS traffic and validate HTTPS site certificates is enabled, which meets Contoso's requirements. There are other options available on this page.

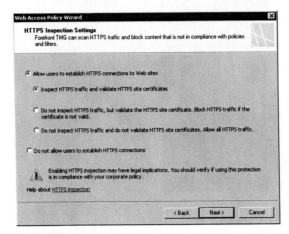

FIGURE 2-43

NOTE For more information on HTTPS Inspection configuration, read Chapter 20, "HTTP and HTTPS Inspection," in *Microsoft Forefront Threat Management Gateway (TMG) Administrator's Companion*, from Microsoft Press.

22. The HTTPS Inspection Preferences page allows you to configure the user's experience when dealing with sites that use SSL. By default, the No, Do Not Notify Users Of HTTPS Inspection option is selected, as shown in Figure 2-44. If you change this option to Yes, Notify Users, only clients that have the Forefront TMG Client installed will receive this notification. The next option instructs Forefront TMG to use a self-signed certificate, which matches Contoso's requirements since Contoso doesn't have an internal CA infrastructure. For the purpose of this example, leave these options selected, and then click Next to continue.

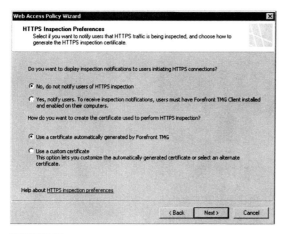

FIGURE 2-44

23. The Certificate Deployment Preferences page appears next. Type the domain administrator username and password, as shown in Figure 2-45. Next, type the credentials, and then click Next to proceed.

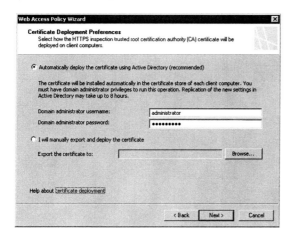

FIGURE 2-45

24. On the Web Cache Configuration page, you configure the size of the Web cache, which for Contoso's requirements should be set to 1 GB. As Figure 2-46 shows, the current configuration is set to zero. Click the Cache Drives button.

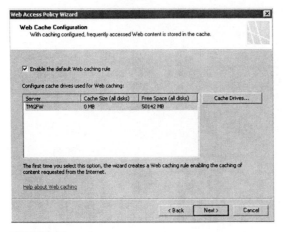

FIGURE 2-46

25. In the Define Cache Drives dialog box, shown in Figure 2-47, in the Maximum Cache Size (MB) text box, type **1024**, and then click Set. Click OK to continue.

FIGURE 2-47

26. When the Web Cache Configuration page reappears, click Next to continue, and then click Finish to complete this wizard.

At this point, guided by a collection of wizards, you have met all the requirements for Contoso's network policy in a single deployment phase.

> **NOTE** If you have setup problems, review the Forefront Setup log file in the %windir% \temp folder. For more information on troubleshooting setup issues, read Chapter 9, "Troubleshooting TMG Setup," in *Microsoft Forefront Threat Management Gateway (TMG) Administrator's Companion*, from Microsoft Press.

Administrator's Punch List

Key takeaways from this chapter:

- To get the most out of your TMG installation, you should plan your deployment based on corporate requirements.

- In most cases, a domain-joined TMG firewall will provide the highest level of protection for outbound access.

- The Forefront TMG Enterprise and Standard Editions provide the same security feature set, but the Enterprise Edition enables array and NLB deployment, as well as enterprise policies.

- The TMG Standard Edition, unlike the ISA Server Standard Edition, stores firewall policy in Active Directory Lightweight Directory Services.

- The TMG Installation Wizard is an improvement over the ISA Server Installation Wizard, and enables you to update your server and install required components automatically before the installation begins.

- The TMG Configuration Wizard allows you to set key settings—including computer name, domain name, IP address settings, and routing table entries—during installation.

- After completing the Installation Wizard, you have the option to create a Web access policy.

Deploying Forefront TMG 2010 Service Pack 1

I n the summer of 2010, Microsoft released a major product update: Forefront TMG 2010 Service Pack 1 (SP1) for Microsoft Forefront Threat Management Gateway (TMG) 2010. This service pack is intended to not only fix some issues that were detected after Forefront TMG was released, but also add new capabilities to the product. This chapter describes the new features, the way to install Forefront TMG 2010 SP1, the way to deploy the core features available in this service pack, and what's coming next.

New Features in Service Pack 1

Forefront TMG 2010 SP1 provides improvements to Forefront TMG in four core areas:

- **Reporting**   Forefront TMG 2010 SP1 changes the look and feel of Forefront TMG reports and adds a new user activity report that can show more detailed information about the pages a user browsed and the URL categories that were requested by the user.

- **Secure Web Access**   One of the main uses for Forefront TMG is as a Secure Web Gateway (SWG). One of TMG's core features, called URL Filtering, is a key component of SWG. Forefront TMG 2010 SP1 brings a new capability, called *URL Filtering User Override,* to this feature. URL Filtering User Override allows users to override the access restrictions put in place by the URL Filtering feature implemented by the TMG administrator.

- **Branch Office Support**   Forefront TMG 2010 SP1 takes advantage of the BranchCache feature that is available in Windows Server 2008 R2. This feature provides branch office users with an improved browsing experience while reducing bandwidth utilization between the branch and main offices.

- **Publishing**   A new publishing wizard supports SharePoint 2010 deployments through Forefront TMG.

These features will be covered in detail in this chapter. However, before we discuss new features, it is important to get more details on Forefront TMG 2010 SP1 deployment.

Planning Service Pack 1 Deployment

Before installing Forefront TMG 2010 SP1 on Forefront TMG, it is necessary to plan the deployment to ensure that it goes smoothly. The installation sequence and prerequisites will vary according to your TMG setup. The overall installation process is shown in Figure 3-1:

Forefront TMG
2010 SP1
installation starts

Forefront TMG
services are
stopped

Forefront TMG
enters into lockdown
mode

After installation, TMG
services will restart
automatically

FIGURE 3-1

In order to carry out the Forefront TMG 2010 SP1 installation procedures correctly, you will need to answer the following questions:

- Which Forefront TMG version (Enterprise or Standard) are you using?
- Are the Forefront TMG firewalls deployed as array members or as stand-alone servers?
- What Forefront TMG role (EMS or Firewall) is the machine providing?

When you have this information, you can determine the installation sequence from Table 3-1.

> **NOTE** Before you apply Forefront TMG 2010 SP1, create a full backup of your current Forefront TMG configuration. You should also have the latest Windows updates installed on the computer on which TMG is installed.

TABLE 3-1 Installation based on the Forefront TMG setup

TMG SETUP	INSTALLATION ORDER	GENERAL NOTES
Single Server	1. Single server installation point	Regardless of the Forefront TMG setup, always run the setup with an elevated administrative level.
Array	1. Enterprise Management Servers (master and replicas) 2. Array managers 3. Array members	Before you install Forefront TMG 2010 SP1 on Forefront TMG Enterprise Edition, you must log on to EMS using the credentials that were used to install EMS during the initial setup process. If you try to install the update using a different administrator account, the installation might fail.

Installing Forefront TMG 2010 Service Pack 1

Assuming that you downloaded Forefront TMG 2010 SP1 in English—from the Microsoft Download Center (*http://www.microsoft.com/downloads/details.aspx?FamilyID=f0fd5770 -7360-4916-a5be-a88a0fd76c7c&displaylang=en*) to a temporary folder, such as C:\temp— start the installation by following these steps:

1. Click Start, right-click Command Prompt, and choose the Run As Administrator option.

2. Type **cd c:\temp** to switch to the temporary folder.

3. Type **TMG-KB981324-AMD64-ENU.msp**, and press Enter.

4. On the Open File – Security Warning page, click Open.

5. When the Welcome To The Update For Microsoft Forefront TMG Service Pack 1 page appears, as shown in Figure 3-2, click Next to continue.

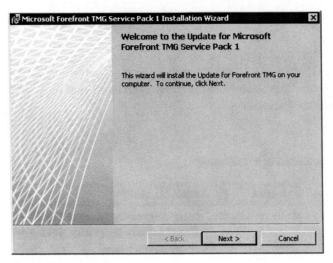

FIGURE 3-2

6. When the License Agreement page appears, read the license agreement and select the I Accept The Terms In The License Agreement checkbox, and then click Next to proceed.

7. The Locate Configuration Storage Server page appears. Because this is the first Forefront TMG to which we are applying Forefront TMG 2010 SP1, the option to specify the configuration storage server is unavailable (grayed out), as shown in Figure 3-3. When you are applying Forefront TMG 2010 SP1 on array members, this option will be available so that you can specify the configuration storage server. Click Next to continue.

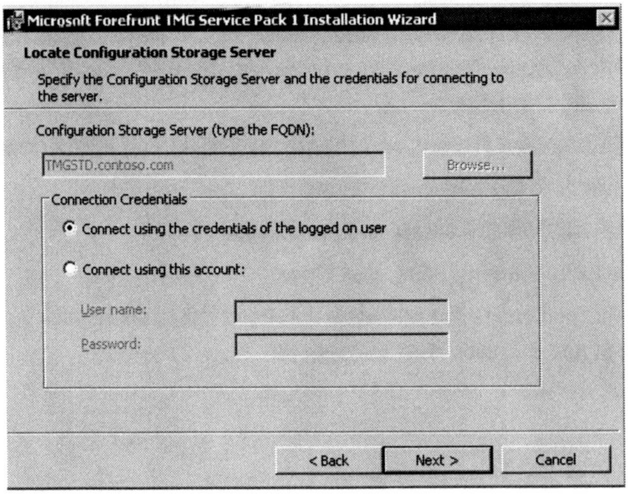

FIGURE 3-3

8. When the Ready To Install The Program page appears, click Install.

9. After the installation is finished, the Installation Wizard Completed page appears, as shown in Figure 3-4. Click Finish to conclude the installation.

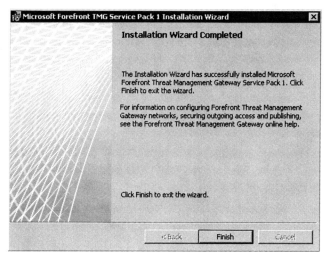

FIGURE 3-4

10. To confirm that the Forefront TMG 2010 SP1 installation is in place, you can open the Forefront TMG Management console, click System, and verify the Forefront TMG version, which should be 7.0.8108.200, as shown in Figure 3-5.

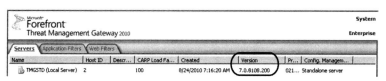

FIGURE 3-5

Administrator's Insight: Troubleshooting an Installation

There are several issues that you might encounter when installing Forefront TMG 2010 SP1, some of which are documented in the Forefront TMG 2010 SP1 release notes at (*http://technet.microsoft.com/en-us/library/ff717843 .aspx#troubleshooting*). There may be other problems with the installation that will require troubleshooting. The general rule of thumb is to start troubleshooting the installation by reviewing the error messages presented in the UI, and then go to the Forefront TMG setup logs to track the root causes of the issues. The Forefront TMG Setup Installation logs are located at %windir%\temp, and the ADAM Setup log files are located at %windir%\debug.

There are two articles on the TMG Team Blog and one on my blog that describe a general approach to troubleshooting installation issues:

- "Troubleshooting ERROR: Setup failed to install ADAM.\r\n (0x80074e46) and 0x80070643 while trying to install TMG 2010" can be found at *http://blogs .technet.com/b/isablog/archive/2010/07/07/troubleshooting-error-setup-failed-to -install-adam-r-n-0x80074e46-and-0x80070643-while-trying-to-install-tmg-2010 .aspx.*

- "Another TMG 2010 Installation failure with error 0x80070643" can be found at *http://blogs.technet.com/b/isablog/archive/2010/07/13/another-tmg-2010 -installation-failure-with-error-0x80070643.aspx.*

- "Unable to install Forefront TMG 2010 – Error 0x80074e46" can be found at *http:// blogs.technet.com/b/yuridiogenes/archive/2010/08/16/unable-to-install-forefront -tmg-2010-error-0x80074e46.aspx.*

Although these articles are not specifically related to Forefront TMG 2010 SP1, they can be used as troubleshooting methodology for your installation process on Forefront TMG.

Configuring User Override for URL Filtering

In a world in which compliance and security policy enforcement are growing trends, having a secure Web gateway that reflects your IT business requirements is a real advantage. One of the pillars for the Forefront TMG Secure Web Gateway scenario is URL Filtering, which directly affects user productivity by filtering traffic to unwanted destinations. A new enhancement to the URL Filtering feature, introduced with Forefront TMG 2010 SP1, allows users to override restricted Web access and proceed on a per-request basis. This can provide a more flexible Web access policy by allowing users to decide whether to access a site that was initially denied to them. This can help reduce help desk calls, especially for Web sites that have been incorrectly categorized.

While this might sound too flexible when the subject is policy enforcement, the fact of the matter is that the user will receive a warning that a Web site being entered is prohibited and that entering the Web site will be logged. This can help to reveal user Internet usage behavior when accessing prohibited Web sites. This feature uses the logic illustrated in Figure 3-6.

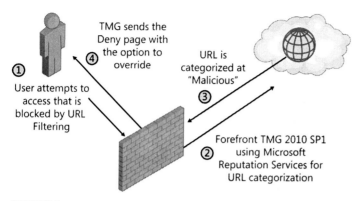

FIGURE 3-6

When Forefront TMG sends the Deny page, as illustrated by Step 4, if the user clicks Override Access Restriction, Forefront TMG will allocate to the user's browser a cookie that will accompany all subsequent Web requests to this domain, and the browser is triggered to reload the URL. Once Forefront TMG receives the Web request with the cookie, it will effectively disable the blocking rule for this particular Web request. It is important to understand that the cookie will remain valid only for the length of the browser session or until the configured time-out period expires. The other important notes about this feature are:

- In order for the user override feature to work, one of the subsequent firewall policy rules must allow access to the requested destination.
- User override configuration requires that you create Deny rules; you cannot enable Allow rules with category exceptions and then enable a user override.
- The user override option only works for the HTTP protocol.
- User override is not supported for HTTPS traffic.
- You can't customize the content type for the user override feature; the rule must apply to all types of HTTP content.

Now that you know how the core functionality of this feature works, the next step is to implement it by following these steps:

1. Open the Forefront TMG Management console.
2. Click Web Access Policy, right-click the rule that denies the traffic to a set of destinations (for this example we will use the default Deny rule created by the Web Access Policy Wizard), and choose Properties.
3. Click the Action tab, and then select the Allow User Override option, as shown in Figure 3-7.

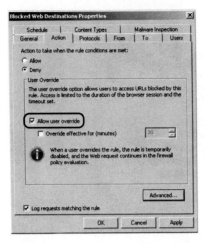

FIGURE 3-7

> **NOTE** You can also specify a range of time during which the user can stay on the blocked URL. This is the time that the assigned cookie will be valid for the user.

4. To customize the error message that the user will receive when attempting to browse a blocked URL, click Advanced. The Action Advanced Properties dialog box appears, as shown in Figure 3-8.

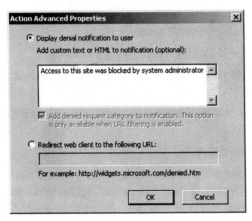

FIGURE 3-8

5. Type your custom message, as shown in Figure 3-8, click OK, click OK again, and click Apply to commit the changes.

Now that you've implemented this feature, you can perform a test using a client who is trying to browse a Web site that matches one of the categories specified on the Deny rule on which the user override feature is enabled. The user will receive an error message, and the Override Access Restriction button will be available, as shown in Figure 3-9.

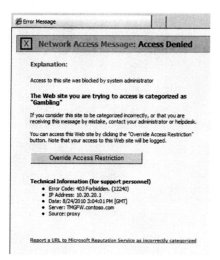

FIGURE 3-9

IMPORTANT   If you don't have an Allow rule for this destination, the user won't be able to access this Web site even by clicking Override Access Restriction.

Reporting Enhancements

One of the most highly anticipated changes in Forefront TMG 2010 SP1 is the enhancement to the reporting feature. The new report design changes the look and feel of Forefront TMG reports, and the new format provides clearer information. Figure 3-10 shows an example of the new report main page.

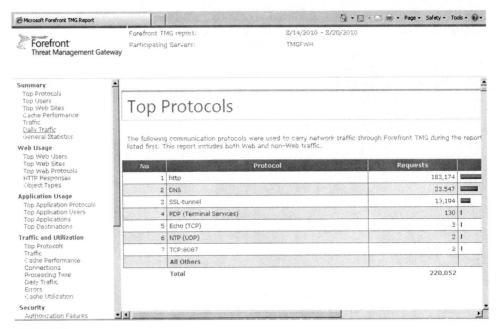

FIGURE 3-10

> **NOTE** More sample reports can be found in "Reporting Improvements in Forefront TMG SP1," at *http://blogs.technet.com/b/isablog/archive/2010/08/15/reporting -improvements-in-forefront-tmg-sp1.aspx*.

The user activity report will contain more granular information about the Web sites that the user visited, including the URL category for each site.

> **NOTE** While writing this book, a Reporting issue was detected after installing TMG SP1. To view the problem and the solution for this problem, review Yuri Diogenes's answer on the following forum thread: *http://social.technet.microsoft.com/Forums/en-US /ForefrontedgeMLR/thread/543b0ef3-68fa-442c-bb3d-a42177809016*.

Branch Office Support

The new Branch Office integration functionality uses a new wizard to help you take advantage of the Windows Server 2008 R2 BranchCache role. This option enables Forefront TMG to act as Hosted Cache Server in a branch office scenario. The Forefront TMG UI dashboard for branch and Web cache utilization can be used for monitoring. To illustrate this feature and the capability to use a Read-Only Domain Controller (RODC) on Forefront TMG, we are going to use the topology shown in Figure 3-11.

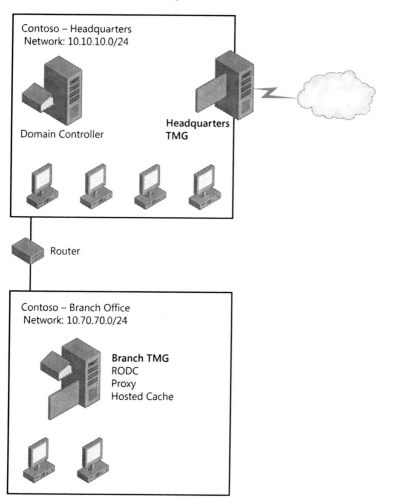

FIGURE 3-11

In order to prepare the RODC you will need to:

- Verify that you have network connectivity to the Headquarters Domain Controller (HQ DC) and that you set the branch server's DNS to the HQ DC.
- If the RODC role is already installed on the server located in the branch office, create a slipstream version of Forefront TMG with Forefront TMG 2010 SP1 to install on top of the RODC. If you try to prepare the RODC without the slipstream version, you will receive the error message shown in Figure 3-12.

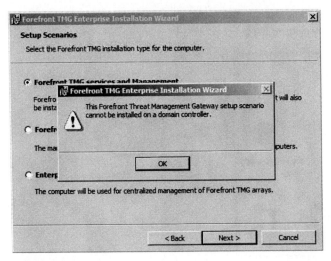

FIGURE 3-12

- Verify that the server located in the branch office is already a member of the domain (in this case it is a member of contoso.com).

- Verify that the server located in the branch office uses the domain controller at headquarters as its DNS server.

- Verify that the certificate that will be used by the BranchCache feature is already installed on Forefront TMG under Personal Store, which is under Certificates (Local Computer). Remember that the certificate must be trusted by the clients that are behind Forefront TMG in the branch office.

With these elements in place, the first step is to enable the RODC role on the server on which Forefront TMG is installed to prepare the forest for RODC. To do that, the forest must be at a Windows Server 2003, Windows Server 2008, or Windows Server 2008 R2 functional level. You must run the **adprep /rodcprep** command on the current domain controller for the domain.

After preparing the forest, you will run the **dcpromo** command on the server on which Forefront TMG will be installed, and then follow the wizard. On the Additional Domain Controller Options page, be sure to select the Read-Only Domain Controller (RODC) option, as shown in Figure 3-13.

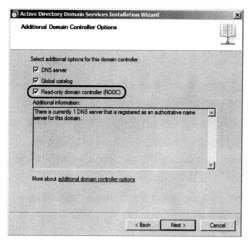

FIGURE 3-13

Continue to follow the wizard to complete the promotion of this server to a read-only domain controller.

> **NOTE** For the complete planning and deployment guide for Active Directory RODC, review the article "Deploying RODCs in Branch Offices" at *http://technet.microsoft.com /en-us/library/dd735411(WS.10).aspx.*

The next step is to install Forefront TMG 2010 SP1 on the server on which the RODC is installed:

1. Run the following command from an elevated command prompt:

   ```
   ServerManagerCmd.exe -inputpath <DVD_path>\FPC\PreRequisiteInstallerFiles
   \WinRolesInstallSA_Win7.xml -logPath C:\Windows\TEMP\TMG-Prerequisites.log
   ```

2. Prepare a Forefront TMG 2010 SP1 slipstream DVD by following these steps:

   - Copy the Forefront TMG DVD and the Forefront TMG 2010 SP1 MSP file to a local drive on the target computer. For the purposes of this example, let's assume this is c:\temp\TMG. At a command prompt, type the following command and press Enter.

     ```
     msiexec /a c:\temp\TMG\FPC\MS_FPC_SERVER.msi /p TMG-KB981324-amd64-ENU.msp /qb
     /L*v c:\tmg\log.txt
     ```

   - Run the upgraded setup program by typing **c:\temp\TMG\FPC\setup.exe** at a command prompt and pressing Enter. Follow the wizard for the Forefront TMG installation. For more information on Forefront TMG installation, review Chapter 2, "Installing and Configuring Forefront Threat Management Gateway 2010."

The Forefront TMG installation automatically identifies that it is running on a domain controller and enables the system policy that allows DC traffic from the internal network to the Forefront TMG server as well as from the HQ DCs (if they are outside the internal network).

Every branch account (user or computer) that is joined to the domain needs to have its password replicated to the RODC for authentication. To replicate the password, complete the following steps on the HQ DC:

1. In the Active Directory Users and Computers console, select the Domain Controllers branch, right-click on the RODC, and select Properties.

2. Click the Password Replication Policy tab, and then click Add.

3. Select Allow Passwords For The Account To Replicate To This RODC, select all relevant local users for this branch, and then click OK.

4. On the RODC's Properties page, click Advanced, and verify that the user accounts you added appear in the list of Accounts for which the passwords are stored on this Read-only Domain Controller.

5. Active Directory must complete replicating the user information to the RODC before you can log on with these accounts.

The next step to configure the branch office Forefront TMG is to enable BranchCache support. To perform this operation:

1. Open the Forefront TMG Management console.

2. Click Firewall Policy, and on the Task Pane, click Configure BranchCache.

3. In the BranchCache window, select Enable BranchCache (Hosted Cache Mode), as shown in Figure 3-14.

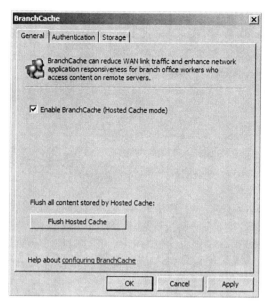

FIGURE 3-14

4. Click the Authentication tab; click Select, as shown in Figure 3-15; and then choose the certificate that will be presented to the client computers for authentication.

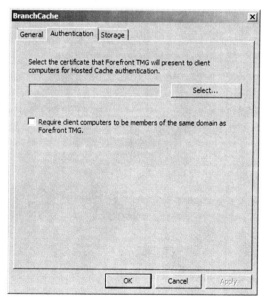

FIGURE 3-15

5. Optionally, you can select the Require Client Computers To Be Members Of The Same Domain As Forefront TMG option if you want to restrict the access to this feature. If Forefront TMG is in a workgroup, you should not use this option.

6. Click OK to continue, and then click Apply to commit the changes.

What's Next?

At the time we were writing this chapter, the Forefront TMG product team was finalizing the next update (post-SP1) for Forefront TMG; it is called Update 1. Update 1 will include some additions to the product, such as:

- **SafeSearch** This is a feature that acts as an automated adult-oriented-content filter in Web search engines, such as Bing and Yahoo. SafeSearch is activated by the end user from a search Web page. Forefront TMG can be used for SafeSearch enforcement when organizational policy requires that all or some of its personnel perform SafeSearch only.

> **NOTE** For more information about the SafeSearch feature, read *http://blogs.technet .com/b/isablog/archive/2010/09/21/new-in-forefront-tmg-update-1-safesearch -enforcement.aspx*.

- **Multiple Categories for URL Filter** This capability provides a way of categorizing multiple categories in a single URL. With this feature, a Forefront TMG Administrator will be able to create access rules that consider all categories returned by Microsoft Reputation Services. An example of usability of this option is: a site can be categorized as primarily a "general business" site, but also as a "Web mail" site. In this case, the "general business" category is ranked higher than the "Web mail" category. So, for example, if a Forefront TMG Administrator wanted to block Web mail, but couldn't with Forefront TMG 2010 SP1 because a site's primary category was general business, the multiple categories feature of Update 1 will allow the Web mail to be blocked.

> **NOTE** For more information about the Multiple URL Categories feature, read *http://blogs.technet.com/b/isablog/archive/2010/09/21/new-in-forefront-tmg-update -1-multiple-url-categories.aspx*.

- **Improve Support of User Account Control in Patch Installation and Uninstallation** Update 1 will include improvements in the installation and uninstallation processes to provide a better product experience in scenarios in which User Account Control (UAC) is enabled.

Beyond these core changes, other minor changes will be included in Update 1.

Administrator's Punch List

In this chapter, you learned about the new features of Forefront TMG 2010 SP1 and how to configure those features, you learned about the enhancements included in Forefront TMG 2010 SP1, and you heard about what's coming next with Update 1. When preparing to deploy Forefront TMG 2010 SP1, keep in mind the following points:

- Review your current environment before deploying Forefront TMG 2010 SP1. Knowing the current role of each Forefront TMG can assist you in installing this service pack in the correct order.

- In an enterprise scenario, before you install Forefront TMG 2010 SP1, you must log on to the EMS using the same credentials that were used to install EMS during the setup process.

- You will need to use administrative elevated privileges in order to install Forefront TMG 2010 SP1.

- If you have installation problems, review the Forefront TMG installation logs under %windir%\temp.

- When using the URL Filtering User Override option, be sure to review the reports and logs to identify the users who are using sites that were initially blocked by URL Filtering.

- After installing Forefront TMG 2010 SP1, review the new report design, and create new reports based on user activity.

- Be sure to plan the BranchCache deployment before enabling it.

- If the RODC role is already installed on the server on which Forefront TMG 2010 SP1 will be installed, it will not work with the Forefront TMG RTM version. You will need to create a slipstream version of Forefront TMG.

- To prepare for the RODC installation, you must run the adprep /rodcprep command on the current controller for the domain.

About the Authors

Yuri Diogenes and Tom Shinder, the guys who wrote this book, spent a year working together on a series of books about deploying Microsoft Forefront. What follows offers some insight about their backgrounds and careers.

Yuri Diogenes

I started working in the IT field as a computer operator in 1993, using MS-DOS 5.5 and Microsoft Windows 3.1. In 1998, I moved to a Microsoft Partner, where I was an instructor for computer classes and wrote internal training materials for products such as Microsoft Windows NT 4 and Networking Essentials. Part of my job in that company was also to maintain the email server (Exchange 4) and the Internet security connection, using Microsoft Proxy 2.0 and Cisco routers. In 1999, I moved to another Microsoft Partner to be part of a team that was responsible for maintaining the computer network for a major Brazilian telecommunications company. There, I was responsible for administering the core servers, which were running Windows NT 4, Microsoft Exchange 5.5, and Microsoft Proxy 2.0.

After finishing this project, I continued working for this Microsoft Partner until 2003 and participated in many other projects involving Microsoft platforms. Before I moved to the United States, I taught operating system and computer network classes for a local university in Fortaleza, Brazil. In December 2003, I moved to the United States to work for Computer Consulting Technologies, Inc. as a contractor to Microsoft in Customer Service and Support for the Latin America messaging division, where I was dedicated to supporting Exchange 5.5, Exchange 2000, and Exchange 2003. In 2004, I moved to Dell Computers, in Round Rock, Texas, to work as Server Advisor on the Network Operating System (NOS) Team, dealing primarily with Windows, Microsoft Exchange, and Microsoft ISA Server 2000 and ISA Server 2004.

I came back to Microsoft as a full-time employee in 2006 to work on platforms (Windows), and I joined the CSS Security Team in 2007 as a Security Support Engineer. There, I started to be fully dedicated to working with ISA. I'm currently a Senior Security Support Escalation Engineer responsible for handling escalations and file bugs for the team that works on ISA and TMG products. I'm also a writer for the TMG team blog and "Tales from the Edge." In 2010, I released my first book, co-authored with Jim Harrison and Mohit Saxena, *Microsoft Forefront Threat Management Gateway Administrator's Companion*, published by Microsoft Press. Tom Shinder was the technical reviewer for that book.

I like to spend my spare time with my wife, Alexsandra, and my two daughters, Yanne and Ysis. We enjoy traveling (mainly on road trips), watching movies, playing on our XBox 360, and making some noise playing our Tama Rockstar drums.

Dr. Thomas W. Shinder

Information technology is my second career. Before entering the world of IT, I was a practicing neurologist who specialized in chronic pain care, headaches, and epilepsy. I went to the University of California at Berkeley and graduated summa cum laude with a Bachelors of Arts in Psychology. I then headed for the University of Illinois School of Medicine and attended classes at the Urbana-Champaign, Peoria, and Chicago campuses. During medical school, I became very interested in neurology and the way neurons were able to use neuro-electrical signals to communicate with each other.

I ended up doing my neurology residency at the Oregon Health Sciences University (OHSU), which has since been renamed Oregon Health & Science University. I then practiced neurology for several years. I realized that medicine wasn't going to be a long-term option for me, as I saw the changes in the wind and knew that the decreasing level of autonomy allowed to American physicians would not allow me to offer the high level of medical care that I was trained to provide. So I had to think about something that I could do for at least the next phase of my life. I had always enjoyed working with computers and, in fact, met my wife, Deb Shinder, on AOL in the early 1990s. She was a police sergeant at the time and was also into computers. So we decided that both of us would change careers and move into the fast-paced and exciting world of computers and IT.

We began with a small consulting firm, not unlike many of those out there who were rolling out Windows 95 and Windows NT to small and mid-sized businesses. Those were the days when we all talked about whether NT would ever take over as the network operating system of choice over Netware. Well, we all know what happened.

Along with our consulting firm, we also began teaching MCSE classes at private technology schools and at the local community colleges. I really enjoyed teaching and often felt that I learned more from the students than they learned from me. There's nothing like the inquisitive mind of a student who's new to a subject, who asks questions that you, as the "expert," wouldn't think of yourself. I learned from the students that you must always continue to ask questions and never take for granted that you ever actually fully understand the technologies you're working with.

A couple of years into my IT consulting and teaching career, I was asked to write a book about Windows. It was quite an honor to be asked to write a book! The first book did quite well, and I went on to write or contribute to over 30 books on Microsoft products and technologies. In addition, I started writing for online and print magazines and have published well over 1,000 articles over the past 14 years.

My real break was when I started working with ISAserver.org, after we wrote our first ISA Server book. The book did remarkably well, and ISAserver.org was a great success. Around 2001, I focused almost exclusively on ISA Server and wrote a number of books and hundreds of articles about it. I also had an active ISA Server consulting practice. I lived and breathed ISA Server for a decade.

Then, in December of 2009, Microsoft asked me to work for them as a Senior Technical Writer on the UAG Anywhere Access Team. What could I say? I said, "Yes!" Now I work on UAG, with a primary focus on DirectAccess. It's a great position, and DirectAccess is the future of remote access. It's fantastic to be on the cutting edge of a mind-blowing technology that will change the way we all work from remote locations.

In my spare time, I enjoy testing out a number of networking scenarios on my Hyper-V servers and then rolling them out on my home office network. That enables Debi and me to "dogfood" a lot of Microsoft technologies. It also helps give me insight into the way things work in production, even though I don't have a consulting practice anymore. When I'm away from the console, I enjoy watching TV, streaming movies from Amazon.com, and watching thoroughbred and standardbred horse races.

What do you think of this book?

We want to hear from you!

To participate in a brief online survey, please visit:

microsoft.com/learning/booksurvey

Tell us how well this book meets your needs—what works effectively, and what we can do better. Your feedback will help us continually improve our books and learning resources for you.

Thank you in advance for your input!

Stay in touch!

To subscribe to the *Microsoft Press® Book Connection Newsletter*—for news on upcoming books, events, and special offers—please visit:

microsoft.com/learning/books/newsletter

LaVergne, TN USA
09 December 2010
208182LV00003B/14/P